Ferdinand Hodler:
162 Paintings

By Maria Tsaneva

First Edition

*****

Ferdinand Hodler: 162 Paintings
*****

Foreword

Ferdinand Hodler (1853 – 1918) was one of the best-known Swiss painters of the nineteenth century. The works of Hodler's early maturity consisted of landscapes, figure compositions, and portraits, treated with a vigorous realism. He made a trip to Basel in 1875, where he studied the paintings of Hans Holbein — especially, Dead Christ in the Tomb, which influenced Hodler's many treatments of the theme of death. In the last decade of the nineteenth century his work evolved to combine influences from several genres including symbolism and art nouveau. He developed a style which he called "Parallelism", characterized by groupings of figures symmetrically arranged in poses suggesting ritual or dance. Hodler's work in his final phase took on an expressionist aspect with strongly coloured and geometrical figures. Landscapes were pared down to essentials, sometimes consisting of a jagged wedge of land between water and sky.

Hodler was born in Berne, the eldest of six children. His father, Jean Hodler, made a meager living as a carpenter; his mother, Marguerite (née Neukomm), was from a peasant family. By the time Hodler was eight years old, he had lost his father and two younger brothers to tuberculosis. His mother remarried to a decorative painter, but in 1867 she too died of tuberculosis. Eventually the disease killed all of Hodler's remaining siblings, instilling in the artist a powerful consciousness of mortality.

Before he was ten, Hodler received training in decorative painting from his stepfather and, subsequently was sent to Thun to apprentice with a local painter, Ferdinand Sommer. Hodler's earliest works were conventional landscapes, which he sold in shops and to tourists. In 1871, at the age of 18, he traveled on foot to Geneva to start his career as a painter.

In 1884, Hodler met Augustine Dupin, who became his companion and model for the next several years. Their son, Hector Hodler, was born in 1887, and founded the World Esperanto Association in 1908.

From 1889 until their divorce in 1891, Hodler was married to Bertha Stucki, who is depicted in his painting, Poetry (1897).

In 1898, Hodler married Berthe Jacques.

In 1908, he met Valentine Godé-Darel, who became his mistress. She was diagnosed with cancer in 1913, and the many hours Hodler spent by her bedside resulted in a remarkable series of paintings documenting her decline from the disease. Her death in January 1915 affected Hodler greatly. He occupied himself with work on a series of about 20 introspective self-portraits that date from 1916.

By late 1917 his declining health led him to thoughts of suicide. He died on May 19, 1918 in Geneva leaving behind a number of unfinished works portraying the city.

Paintings and Drawings

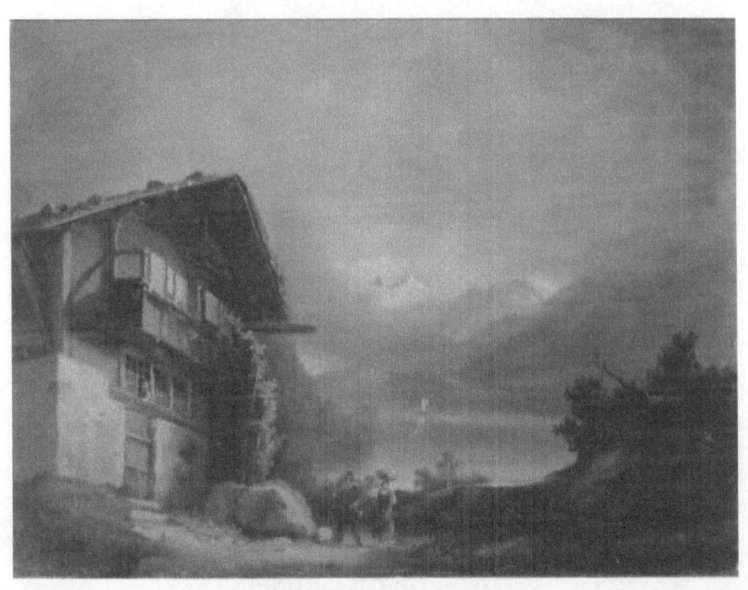

Charlet in Hilterfingen
1871, oil on canvas

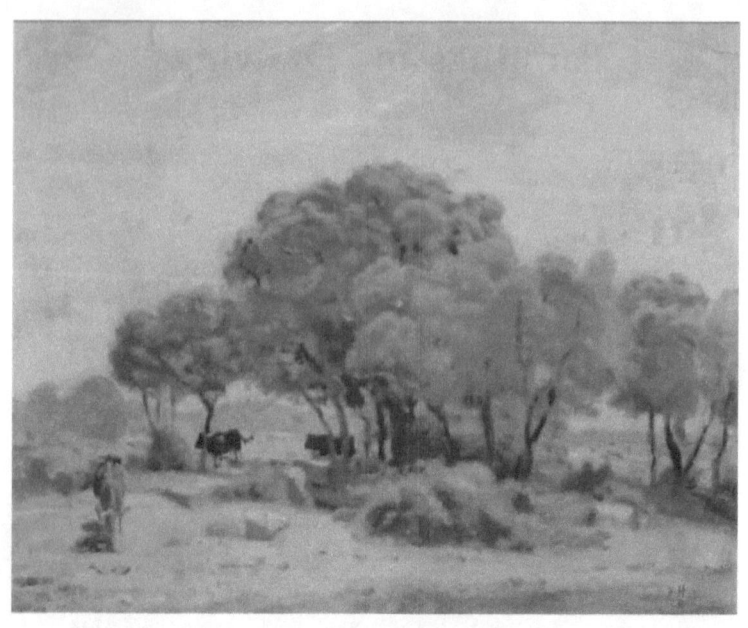

Olive trees in Spain
1878, oil on canvas

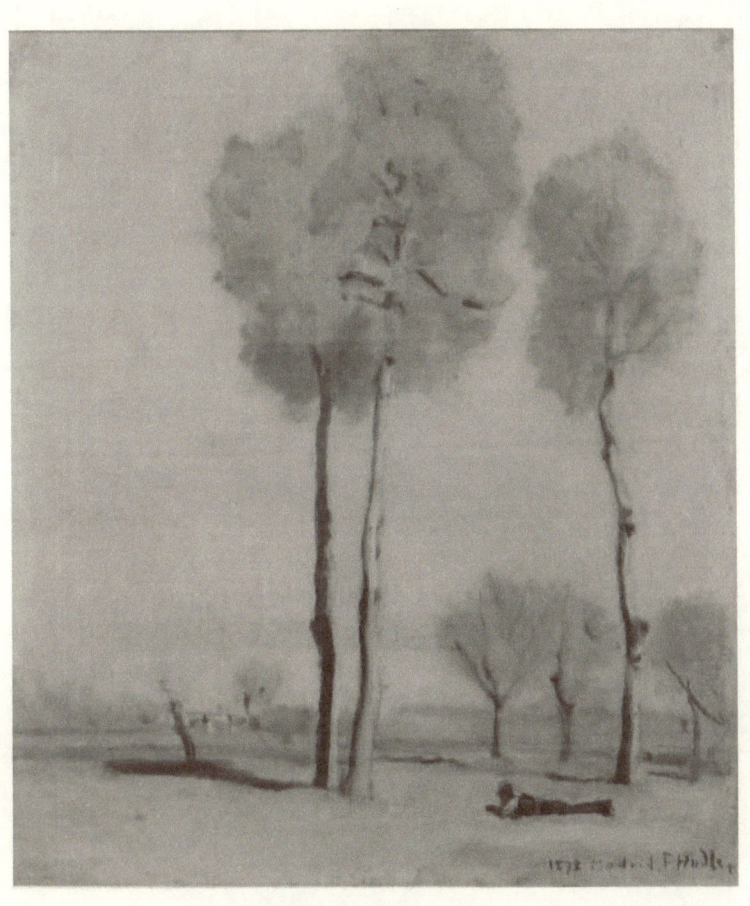

Spanish landscape
1878, oil on canvas

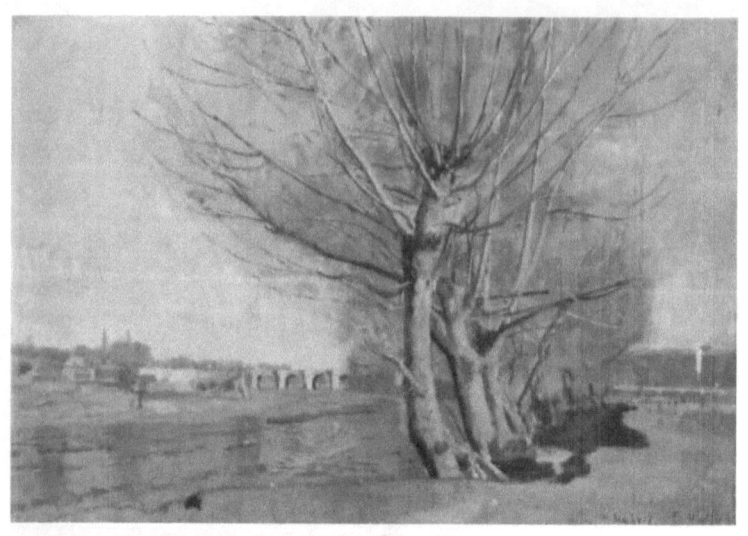

On the banks of the Manzanares
1878, oil on canvas

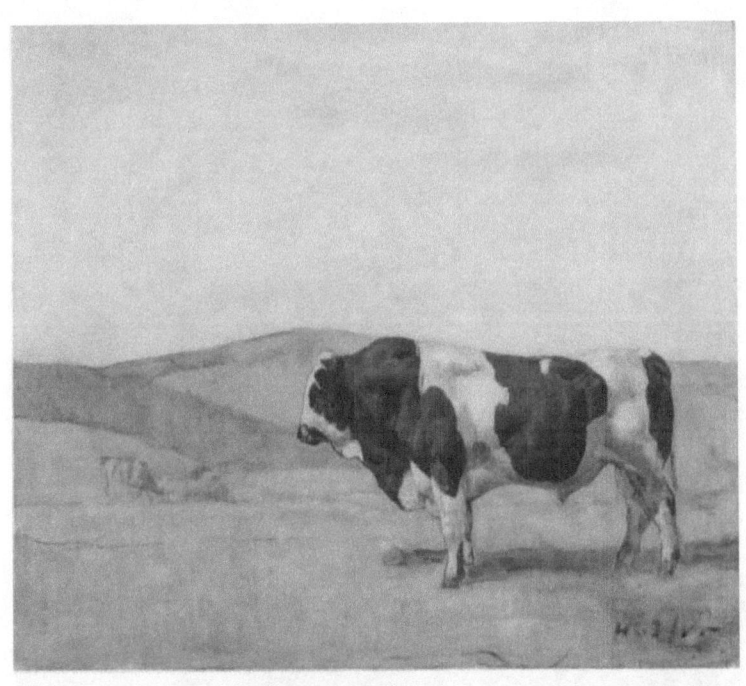

The bull
1878, oil on canvas

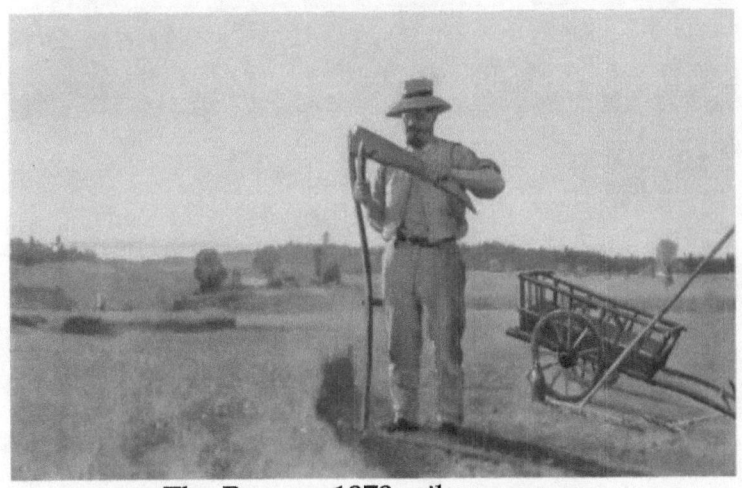

The Reaper, 1878, oil on canvas

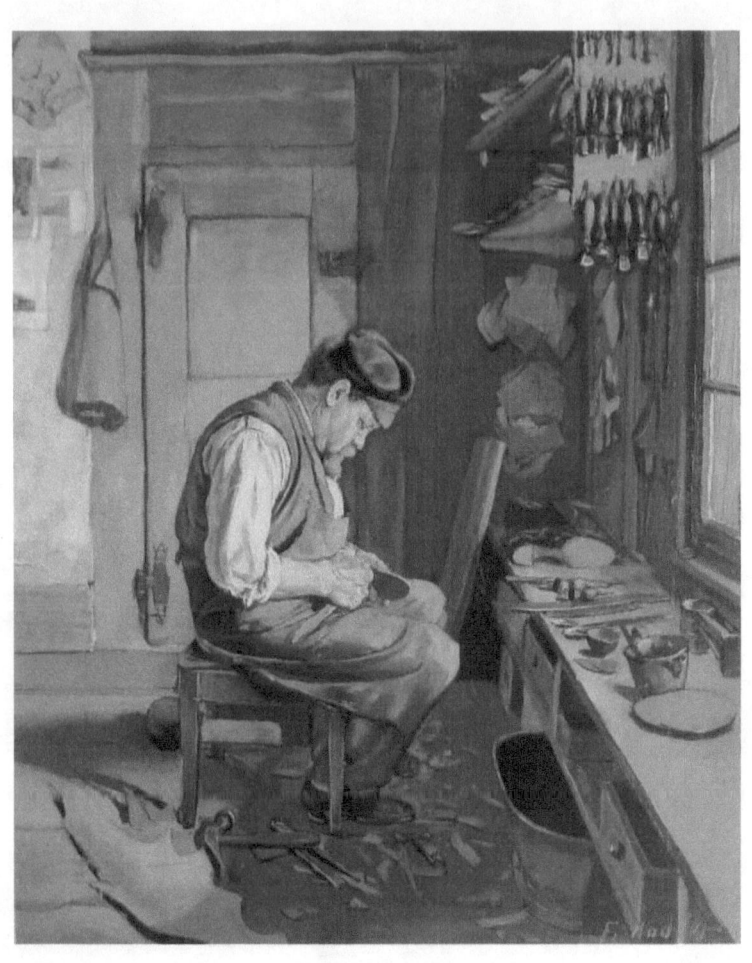

The shoemaker
1878, oil on canvas

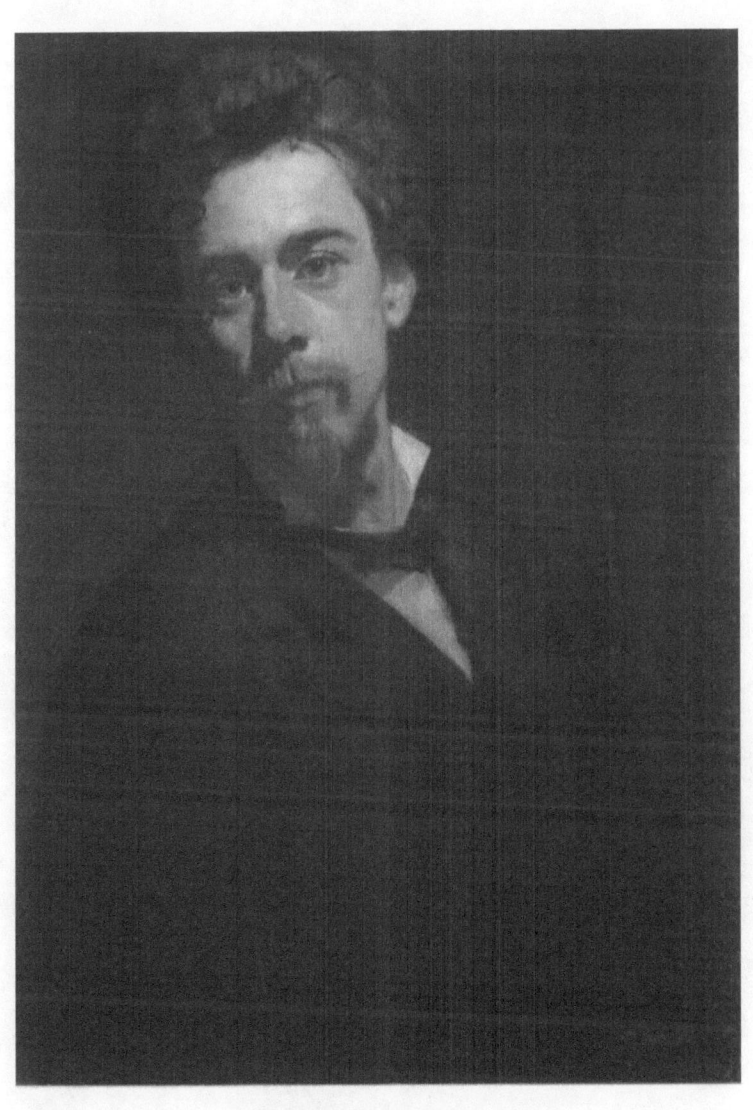

Self-portrait with stand
1879, oil on canvas

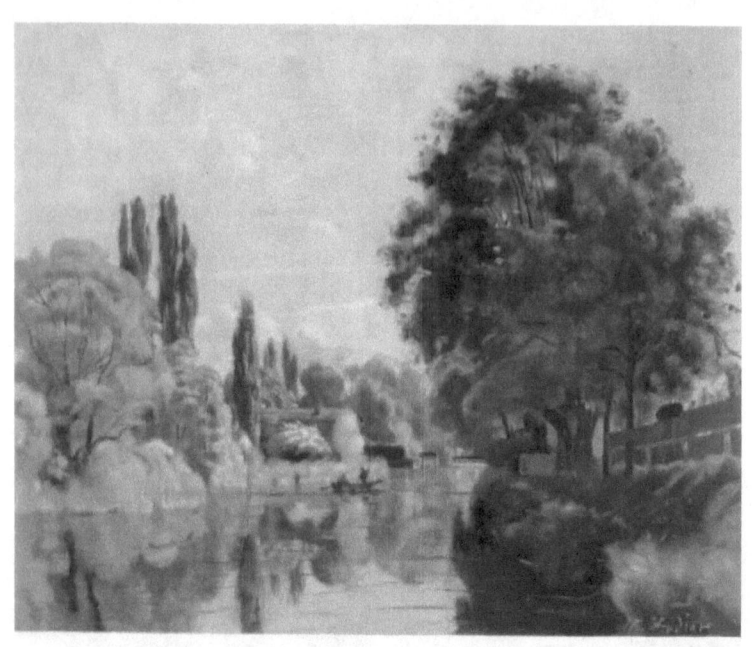

The Aarekanal near Thun
1879, oil on canvas

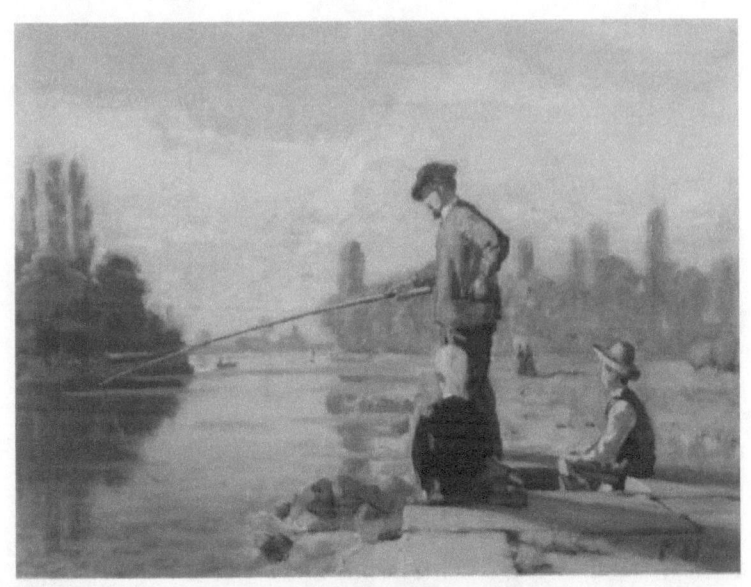

The fisherman
1879, oil on canvas

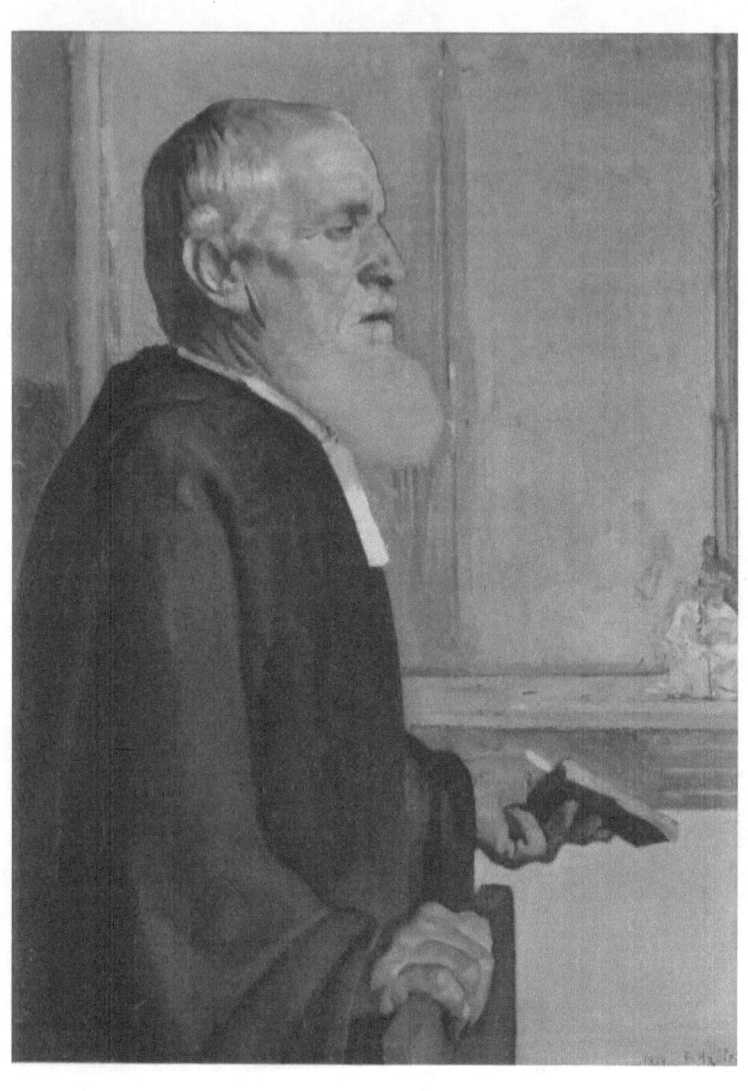

The pastor
1879, oil on canvas

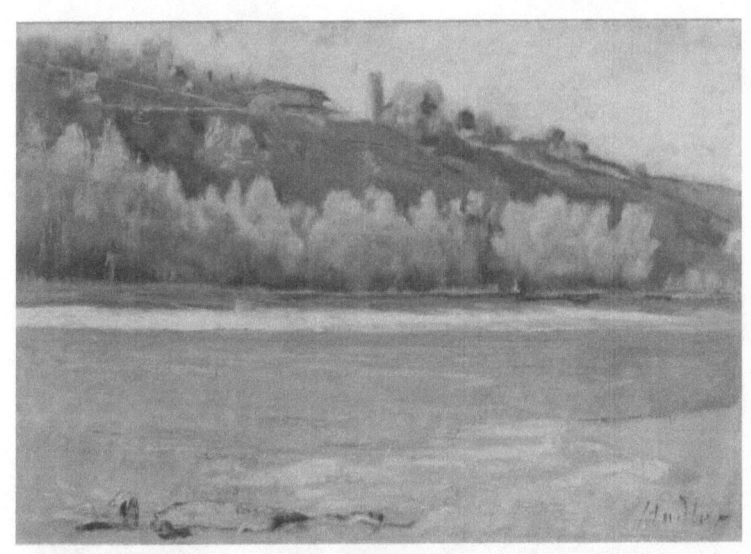

At the Jonction
1880, oil on canvas

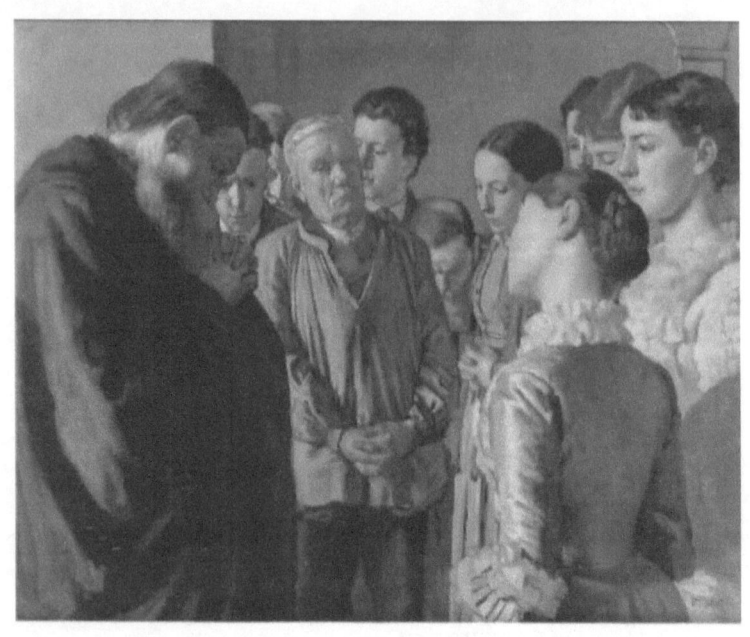

Devotion
1882, oil on canvas

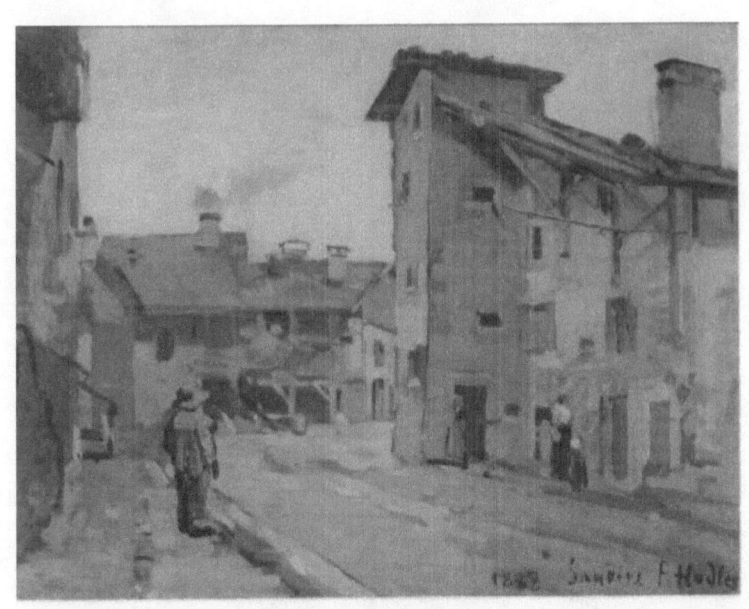

Samoëns
1882, oil on canvas

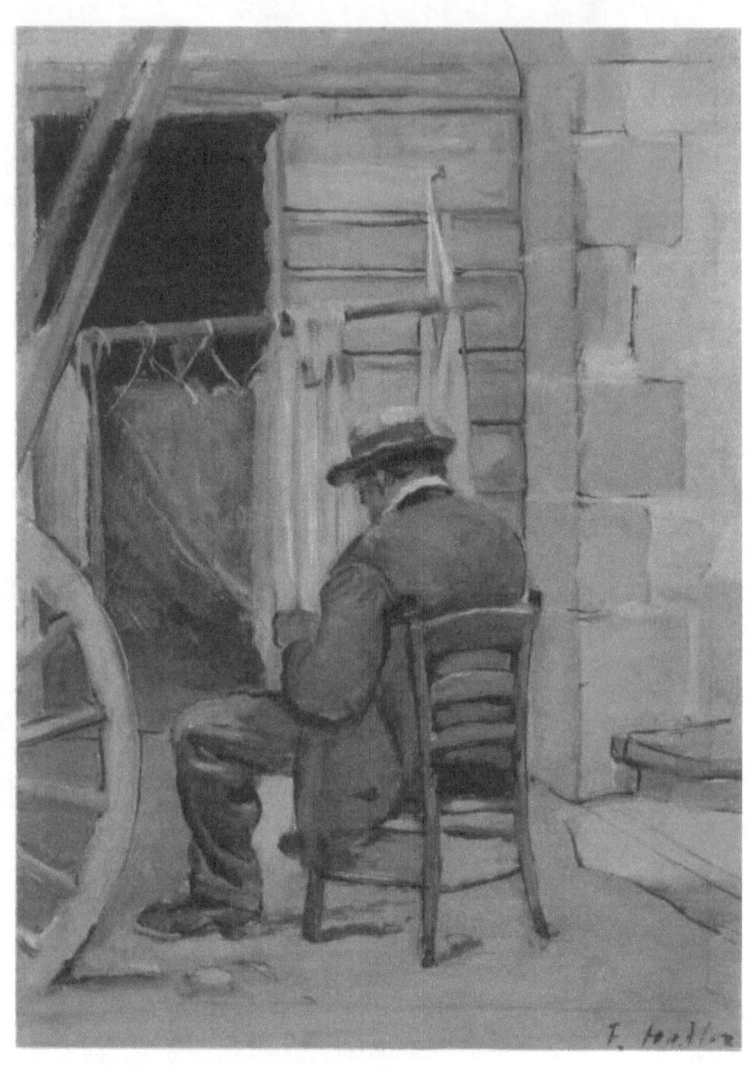

The netmender
1883, oil on canvas

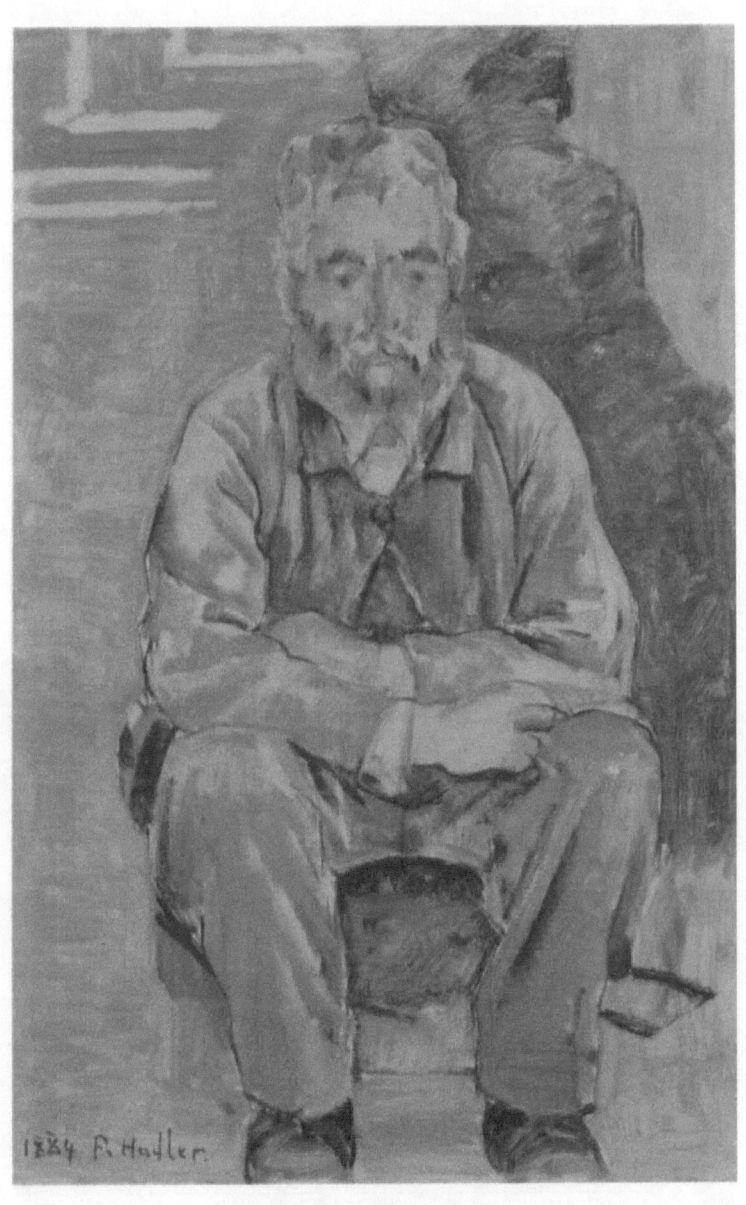

Seated bearded man
1884, oil on canvas

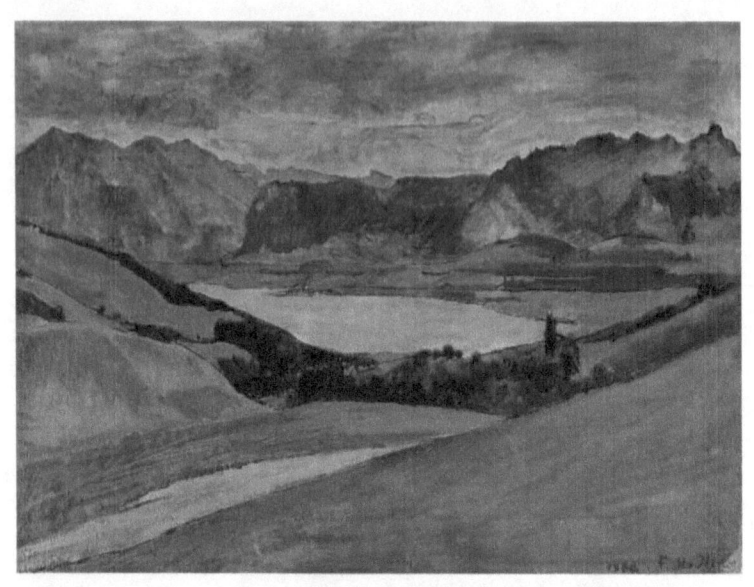

Lake Thun, 1884
1884, oil on canvas

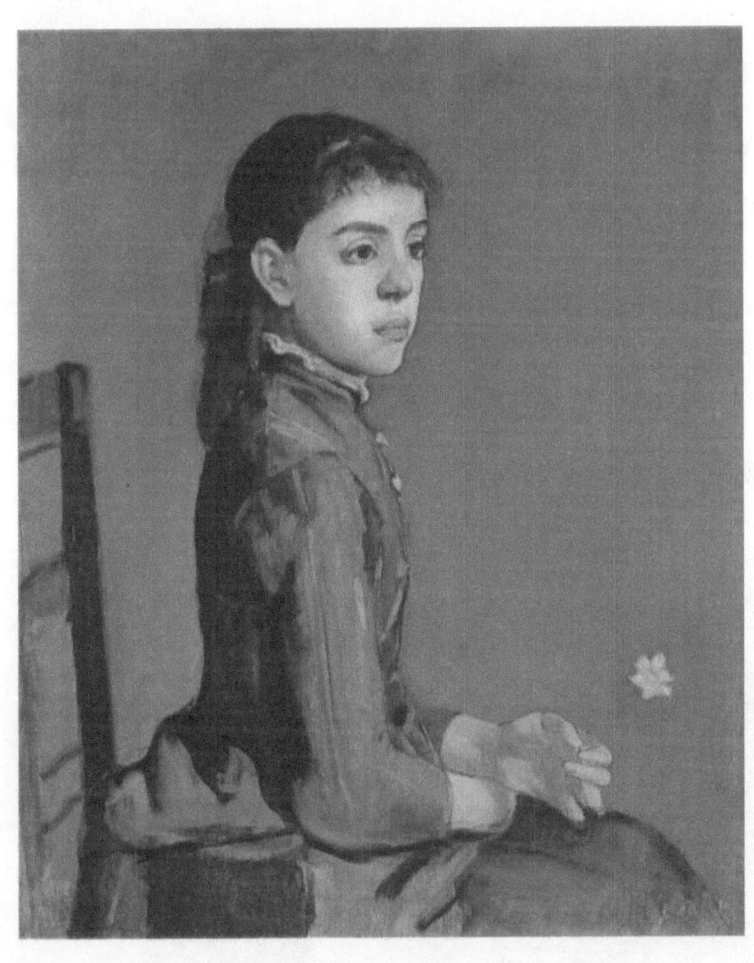

Portrait of Louise Delphine Duchosal
1885, oil on canvas

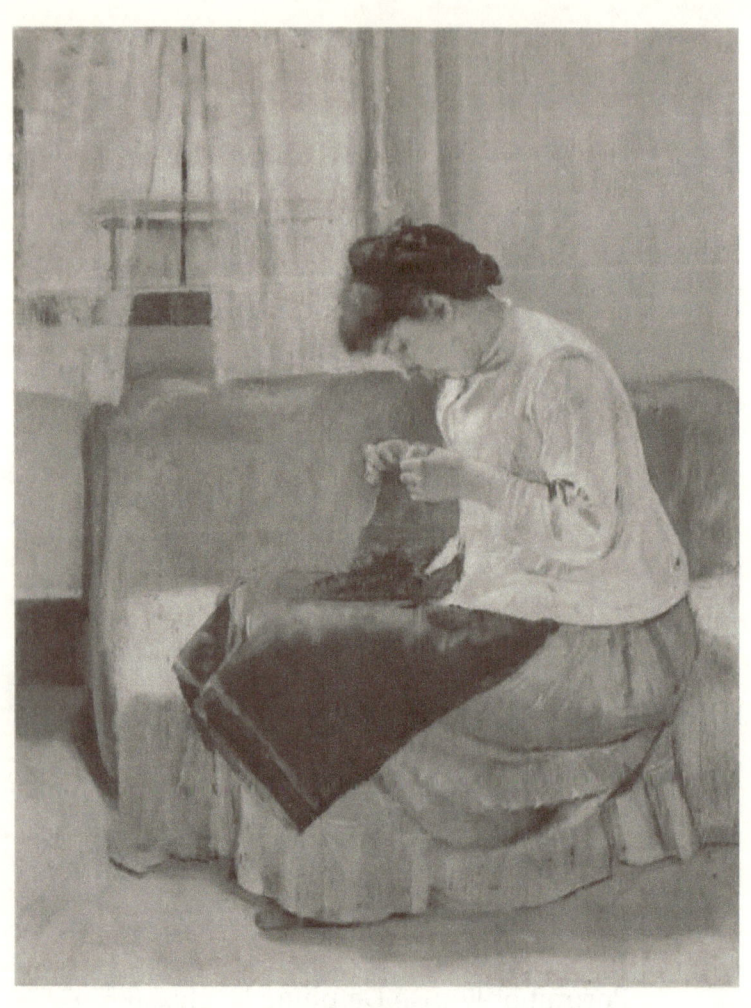

Seamstress
1885, oil on canvas

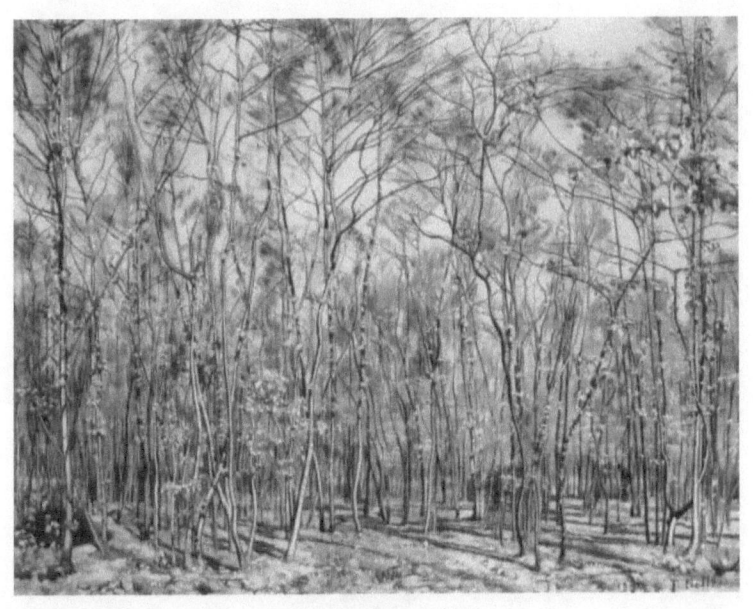

The Beech Forest
1885, oil on canvas

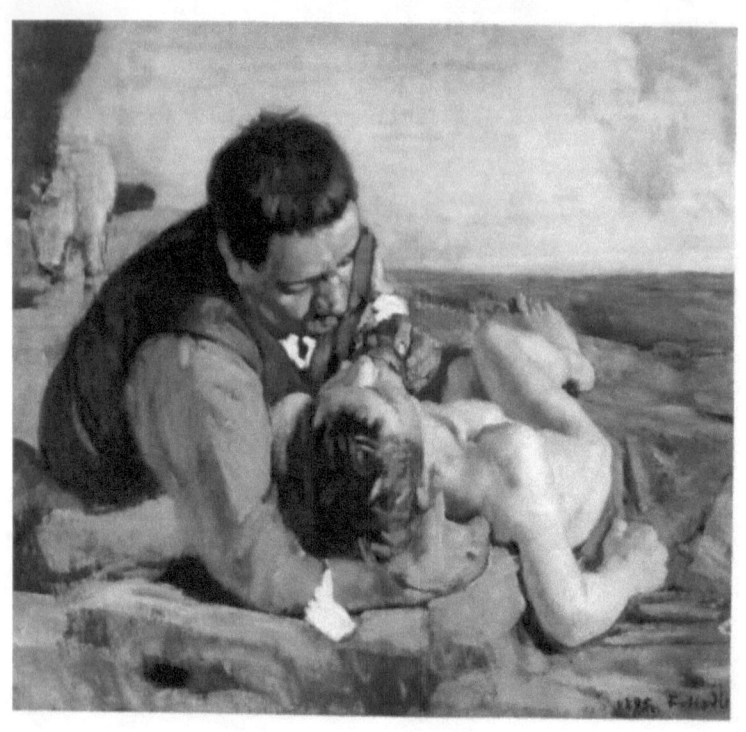

The Good Samaritan
1885, oil on canvas

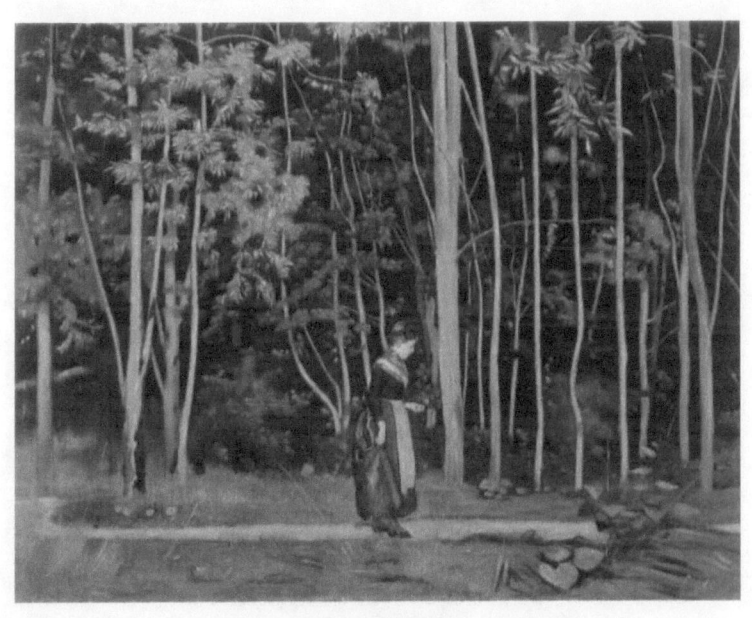

Walking at the forest edge
1885, oil on canvas

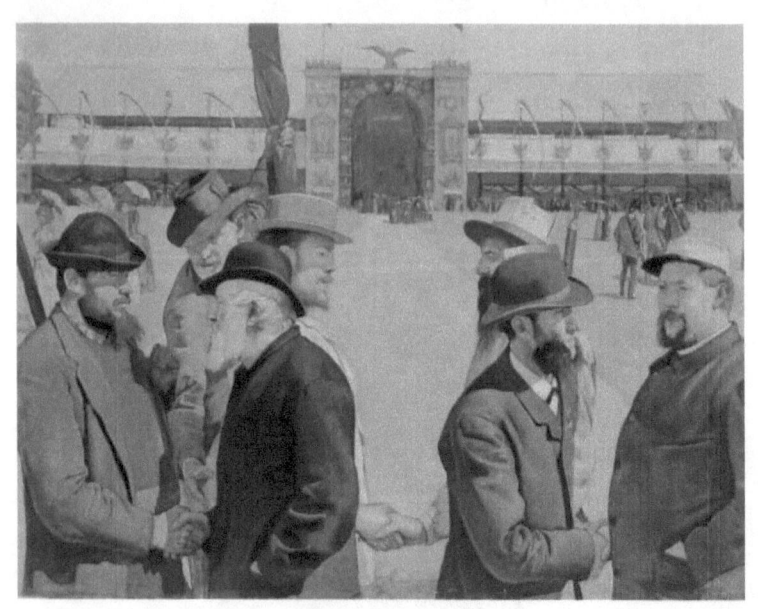

Modern Rütli
1887, oil on canvas

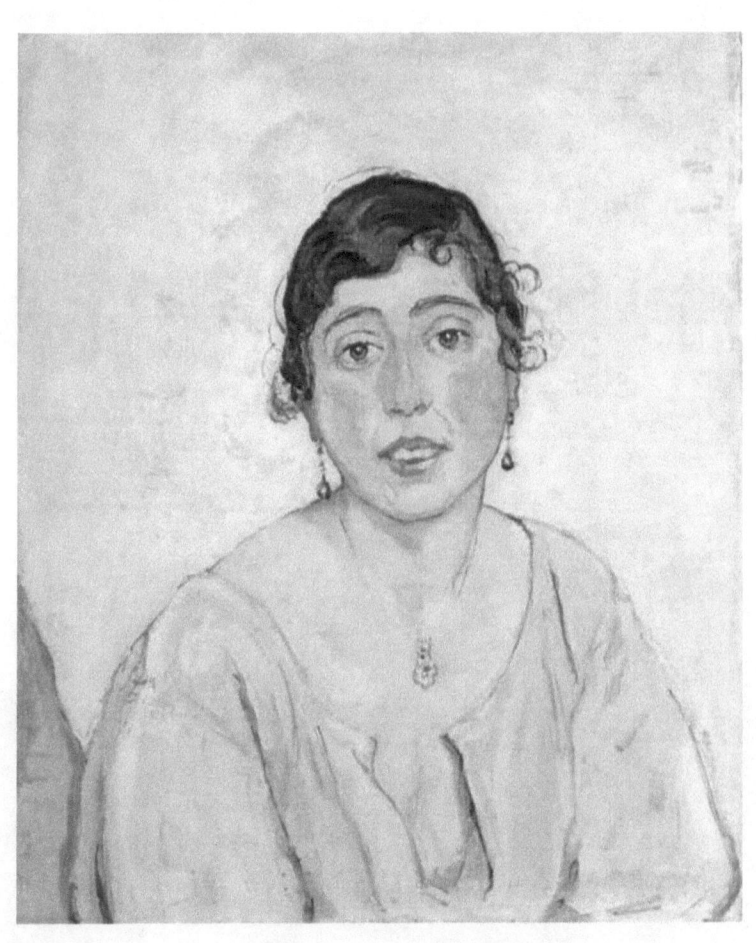

Portrait of a Woman
1887, oil on canvas

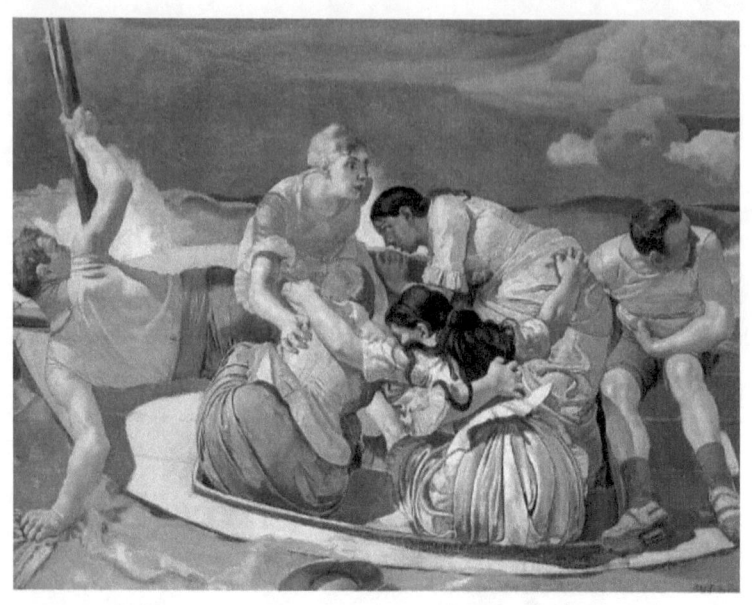

Surprised by the Storm
1887, oil on canvas

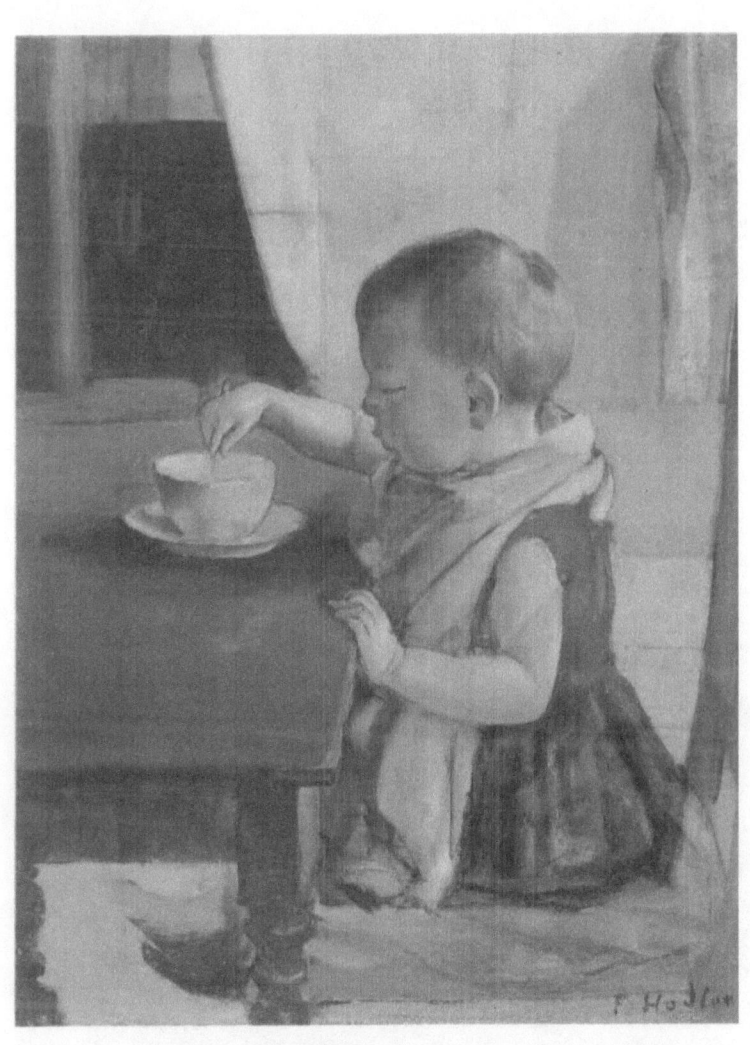

Child by the table
1889, oil on canvas

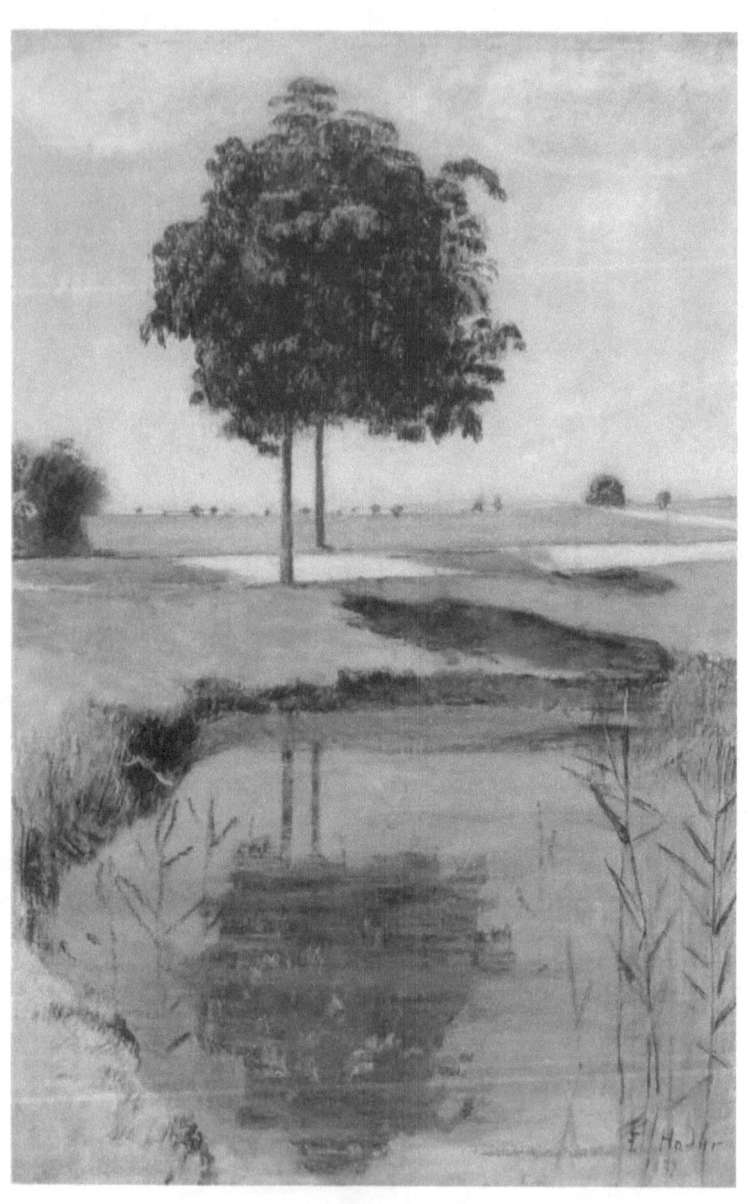

The chestnut trees
1889, oil on canvas

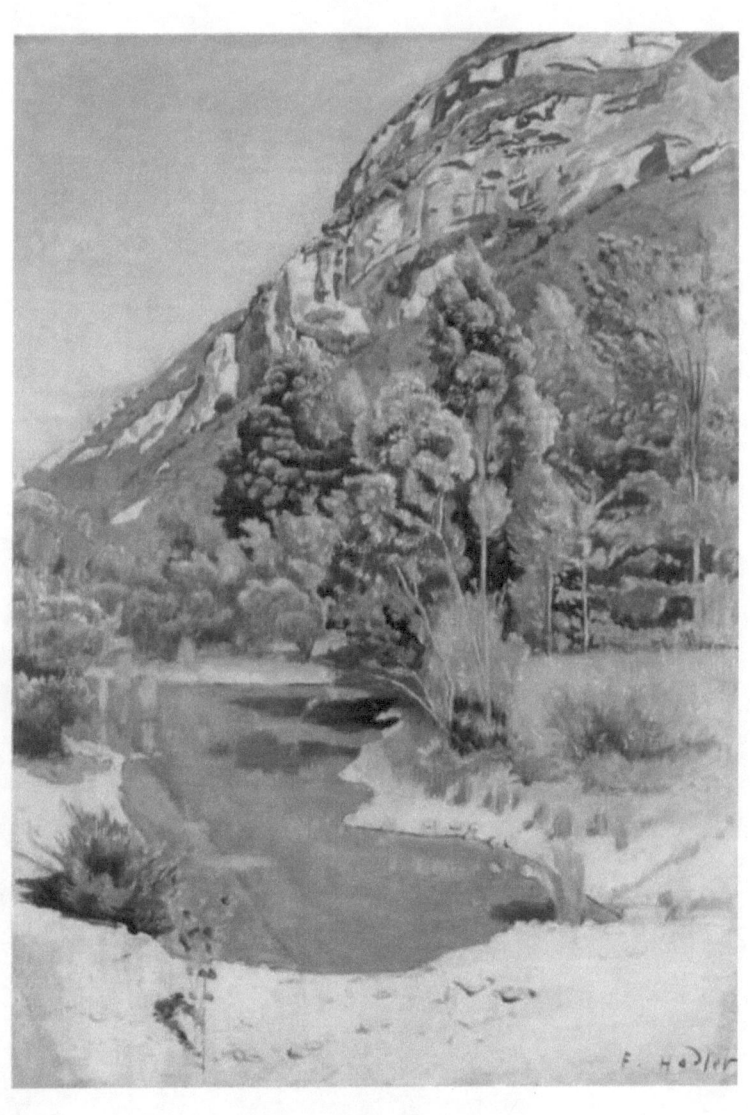

At the foot of the Petit Saleve
1890, oil on canvas

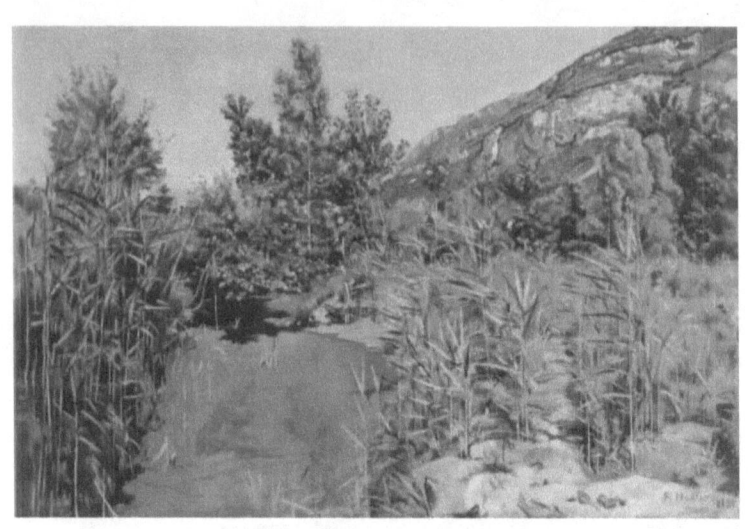

At the foot of the Salève
1890, oil on canvas

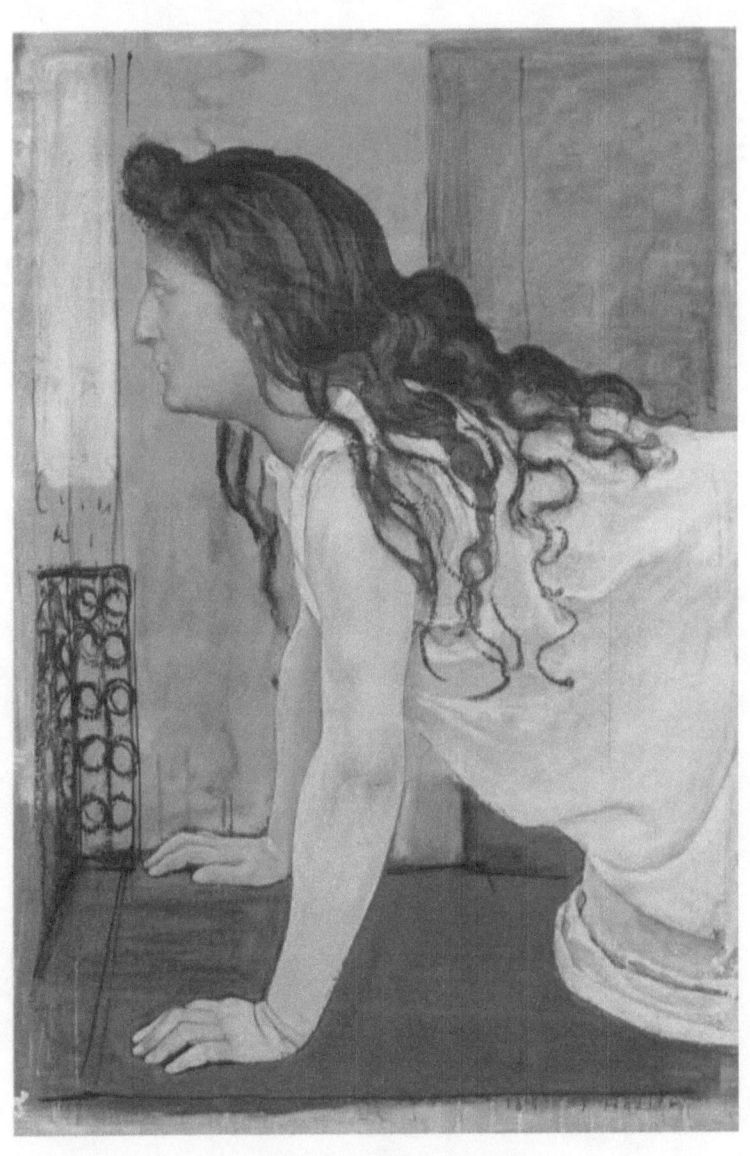

Girl at the Window
1890, oil on canvas

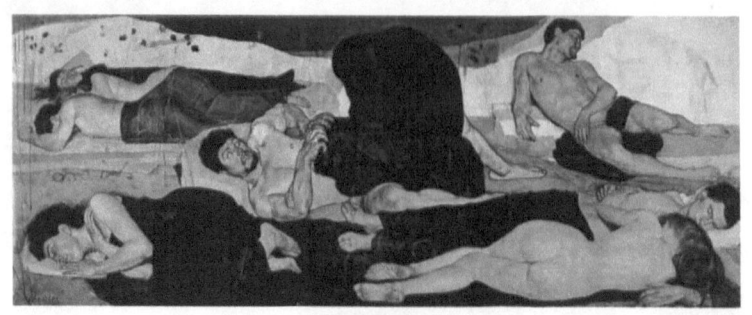

Night
1890, oil on canvas

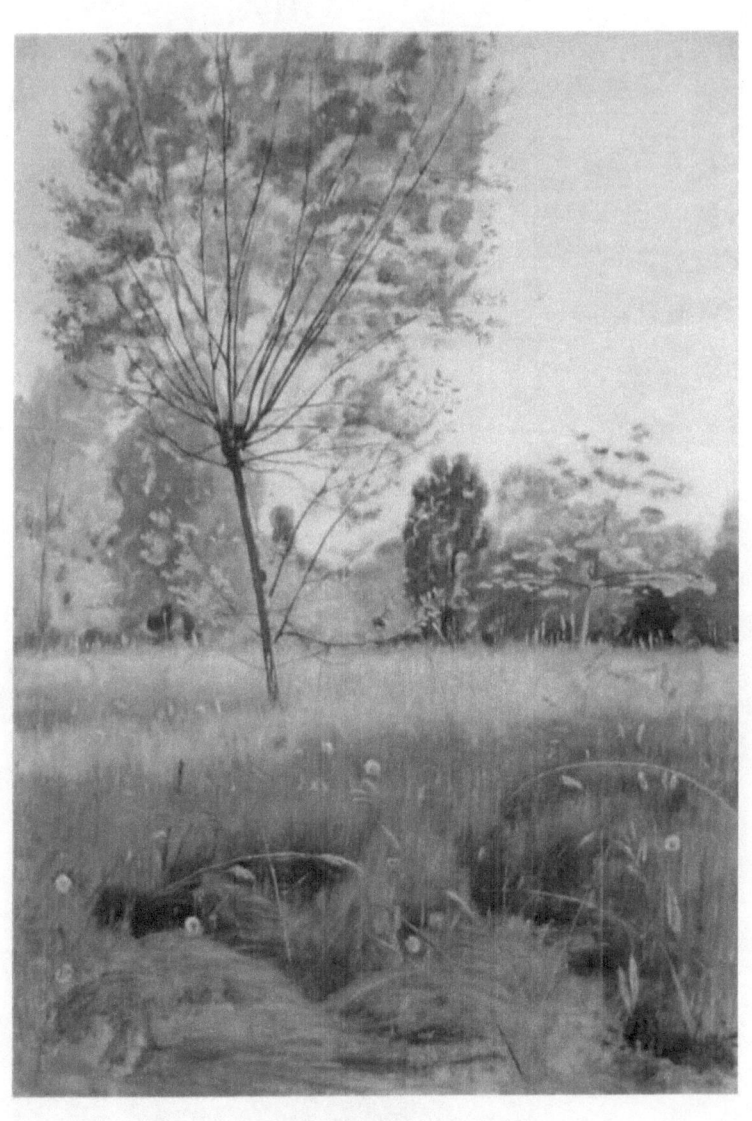

The Golden meadow
1890, oil on canvas

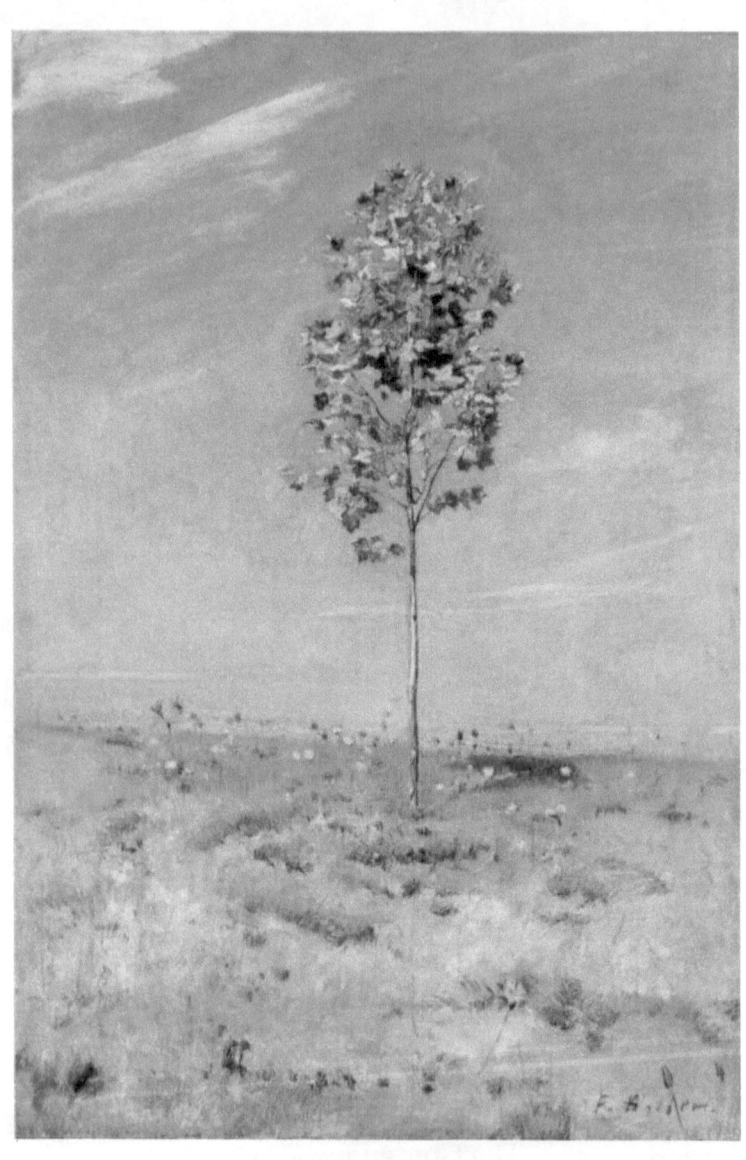

The Small Plantane
1890, oil on canvas

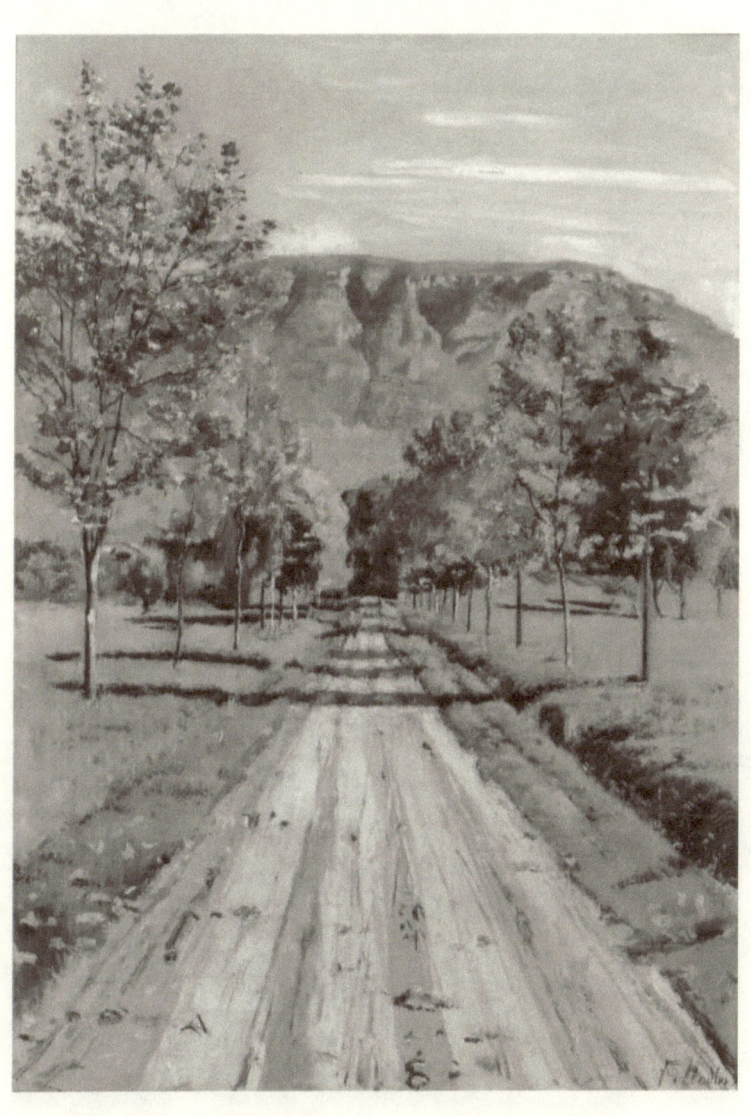

The road to a particular interest
1890, oil on canvas

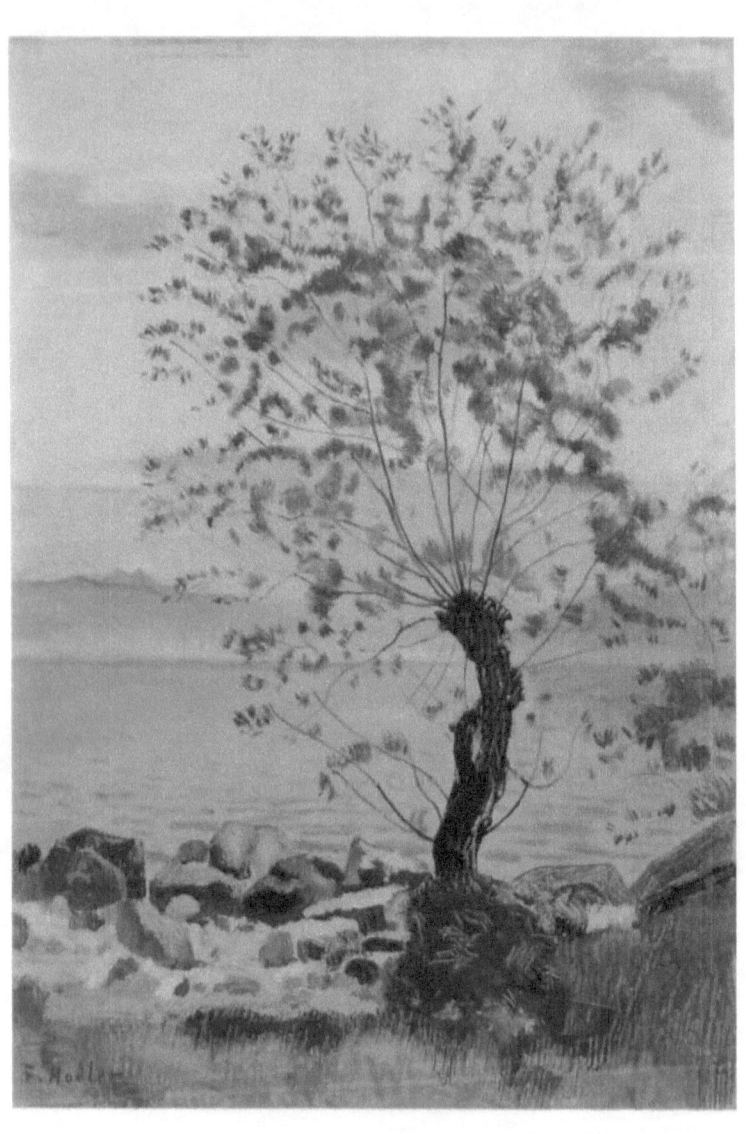

Willow tree by the lake
1890, oil on canvas

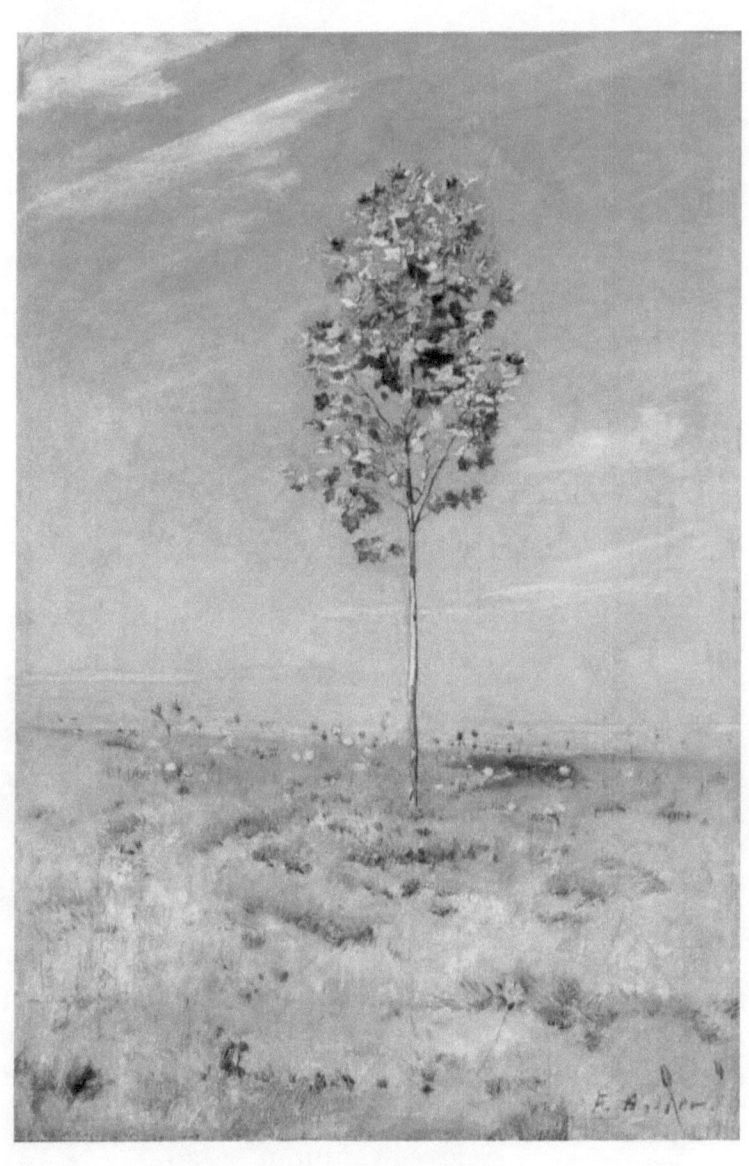

The Small Plantane
1890, oil on canvas

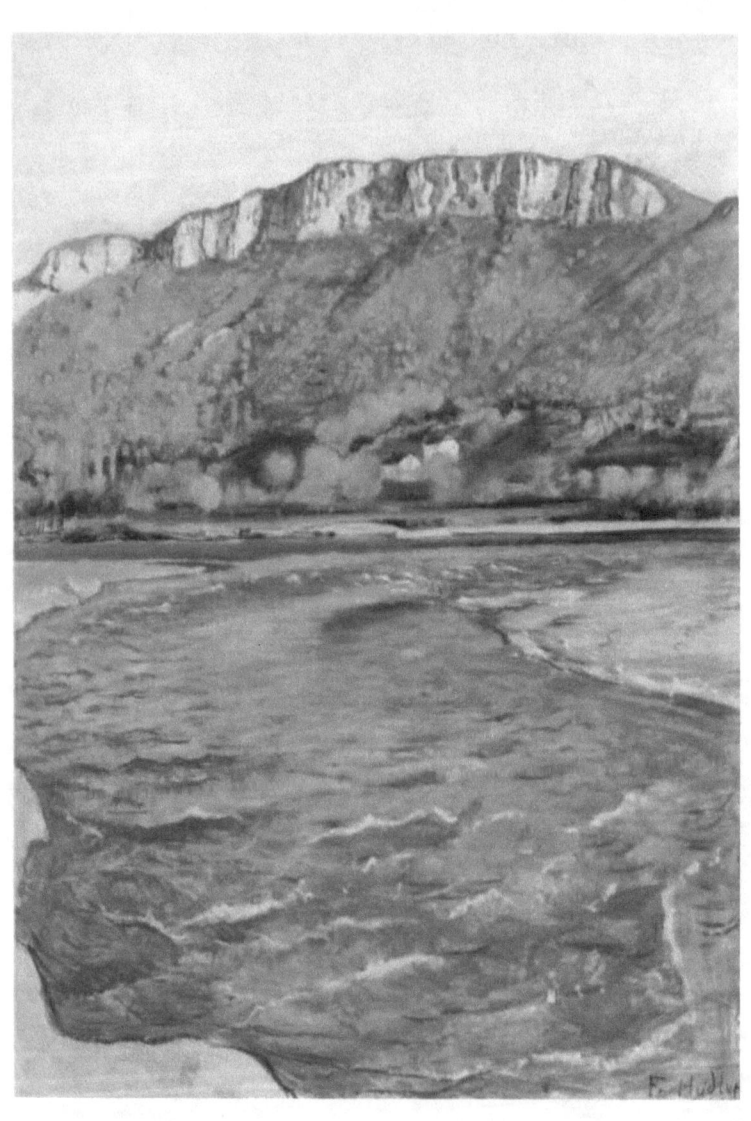

Saleve in autumn
1891, oil on canvas

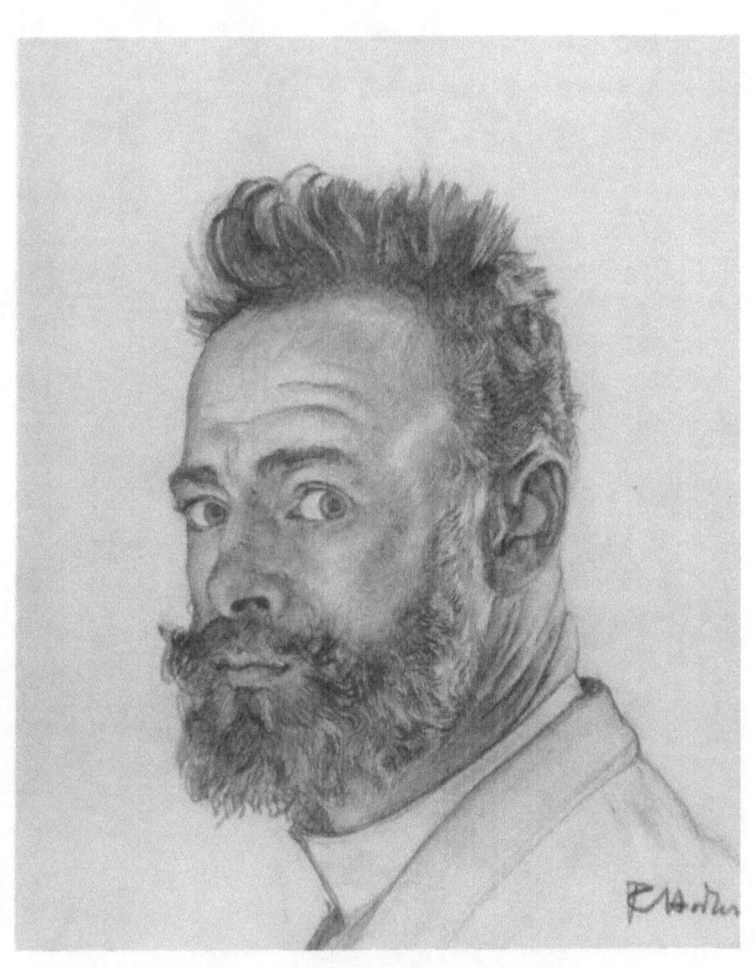

Self-portrait in Paris
1891, pencil

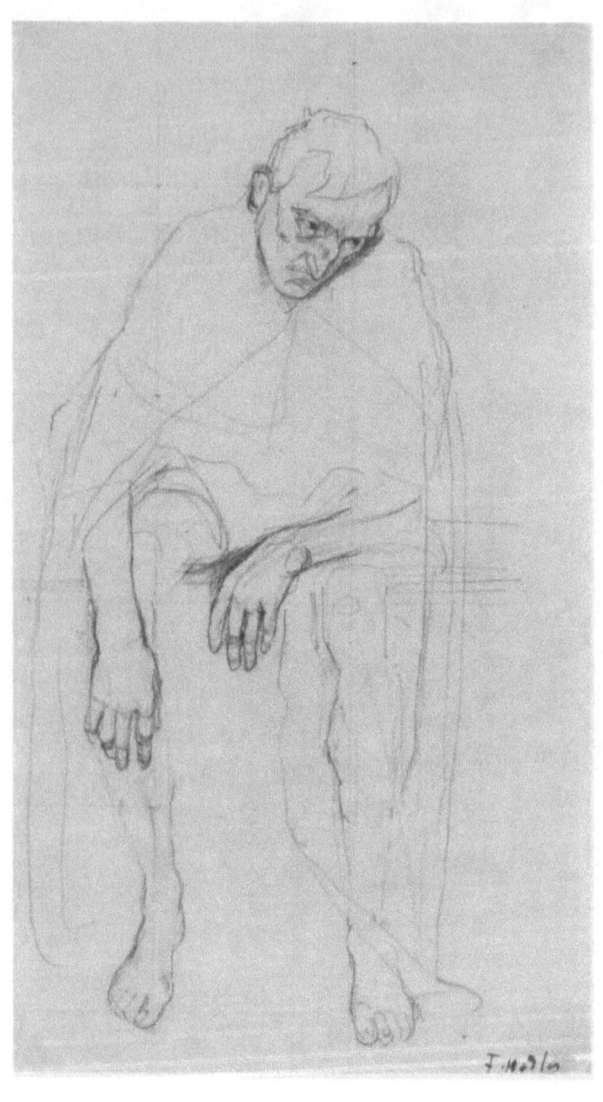

Study of the disappointed souls or Weary of life
1891, pencil

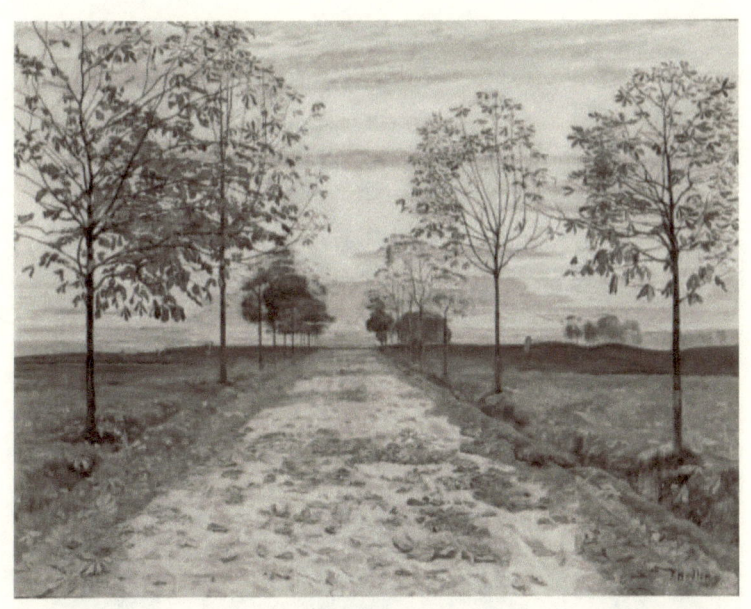

Autumn Evening
1892, oil on canvas

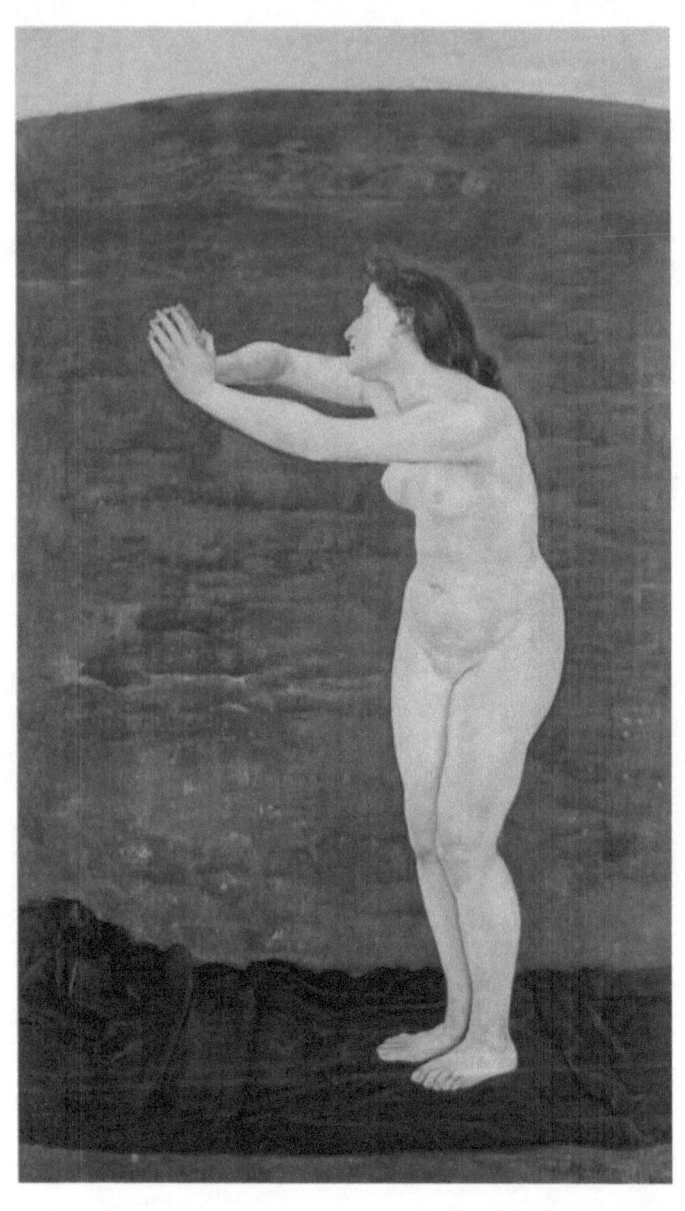

Communication with the Infinite
1892, oil on canvas

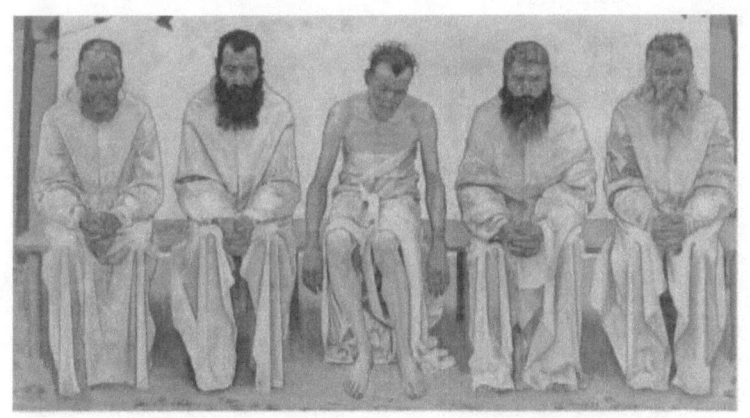

The life of Weary
1892, oil on canvas

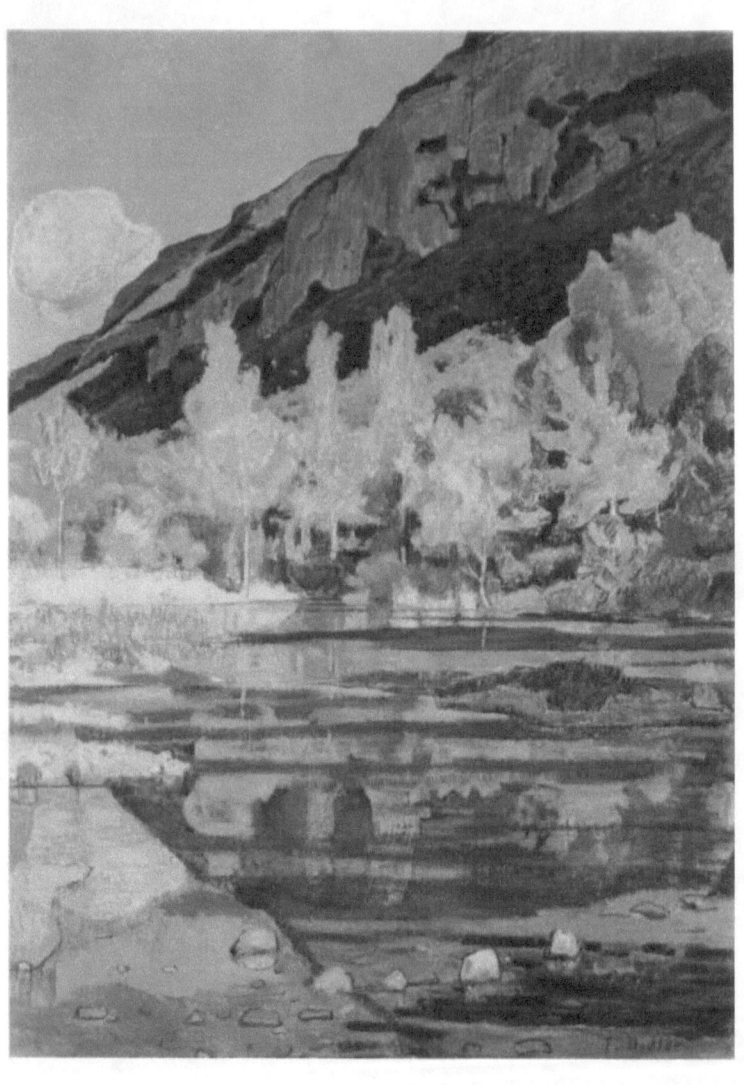

At the foot of the Petit Saleve
1893, oil on canvas

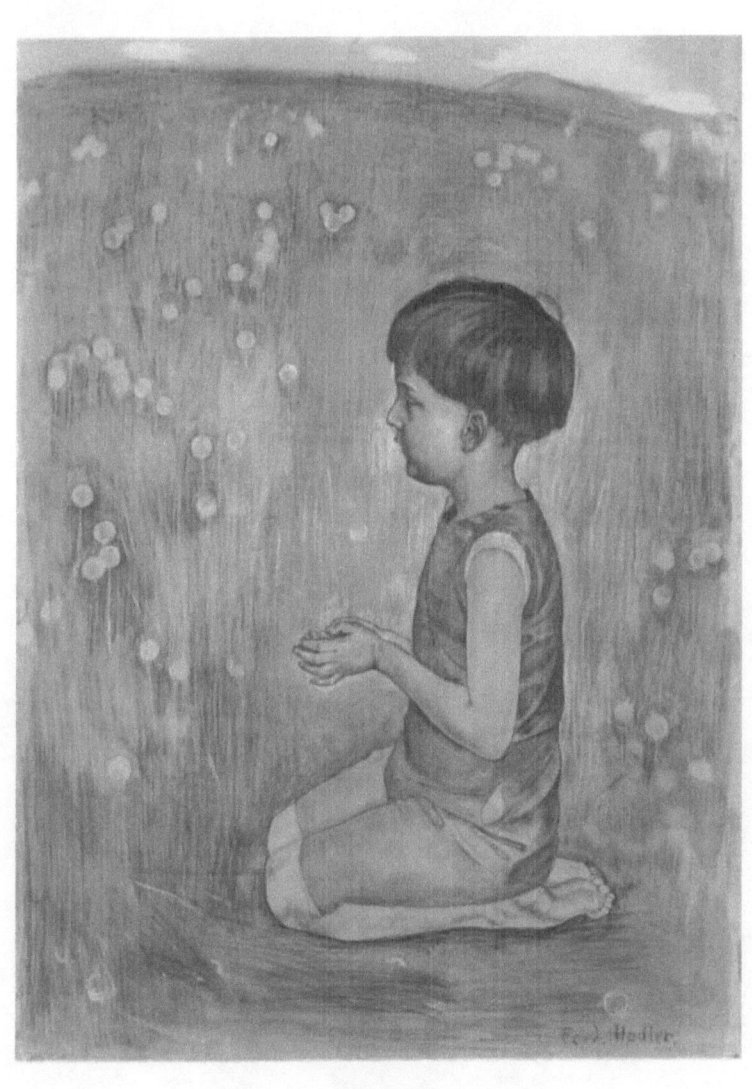

Worship
1893, pencil, chalk, watercolor

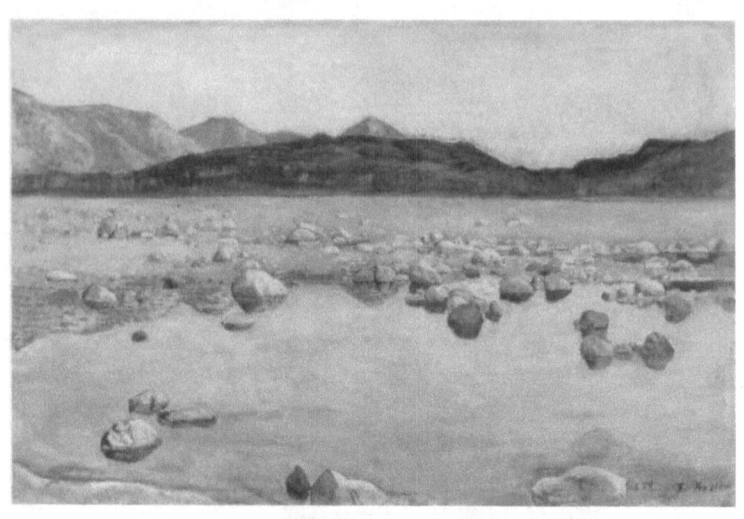

Maggia Delta before sunrise
1893, oil on canvas

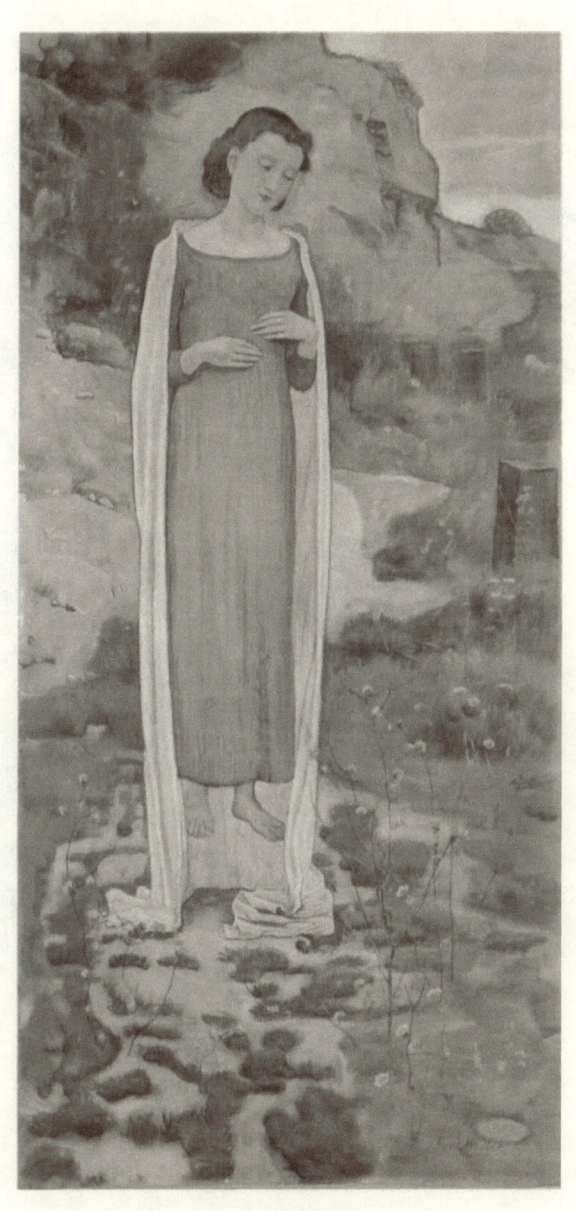

What are flowers saing
1893, oil on canvas

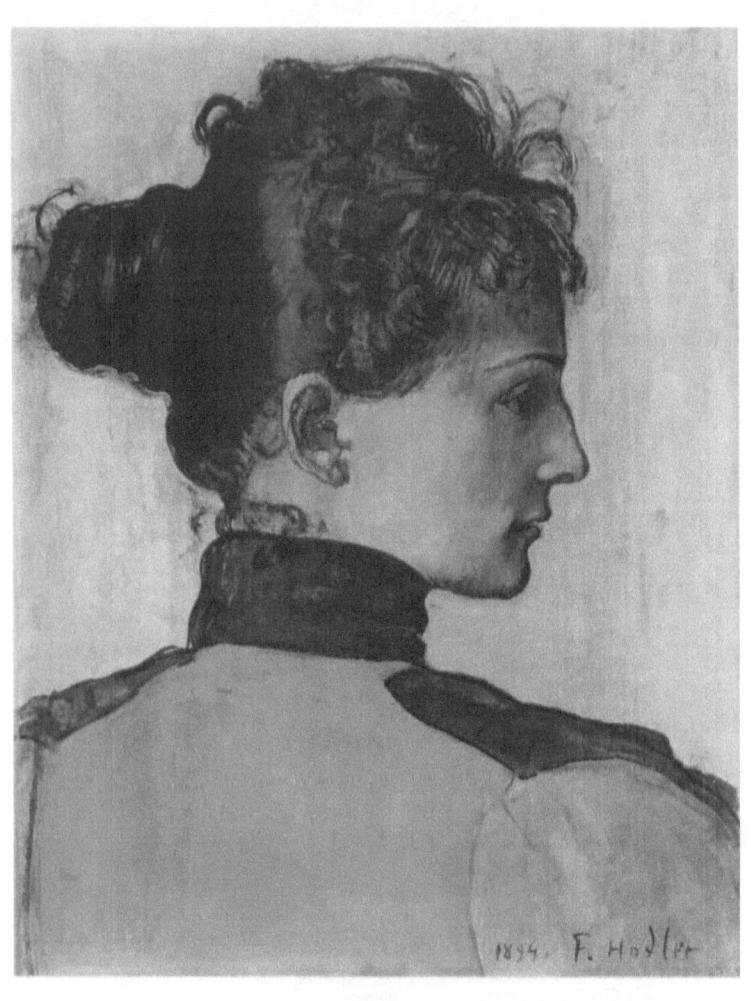

Portrait of Berthe Jacques
1894, oil on canvas

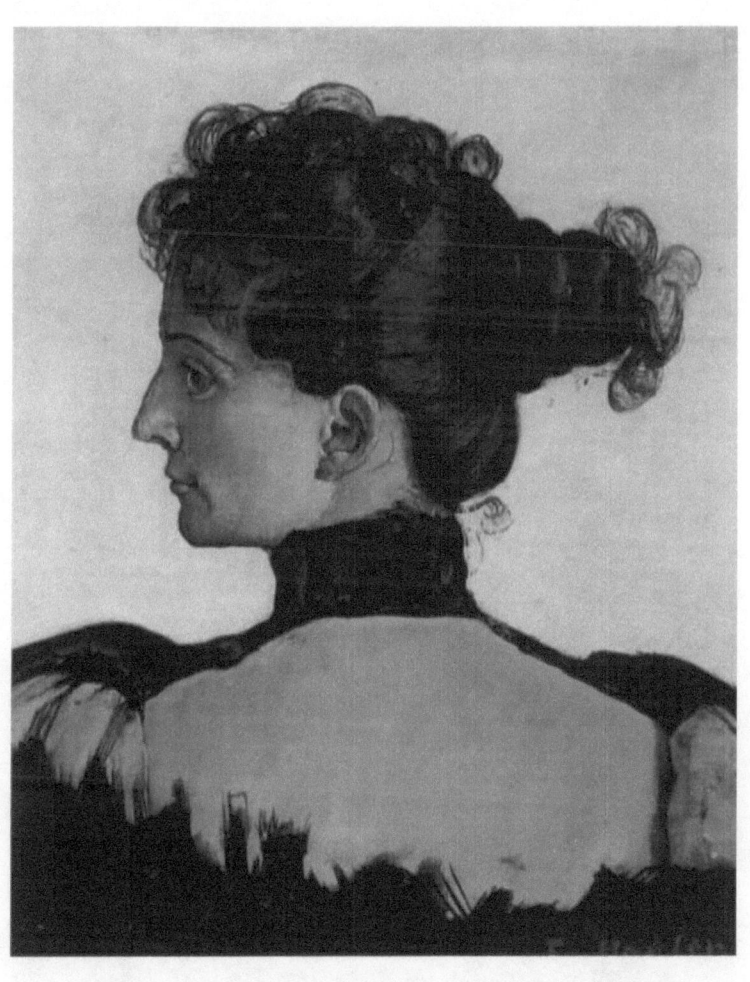

Portrait of Berthe Jacques, wife of the artist
1894, oil on canvas

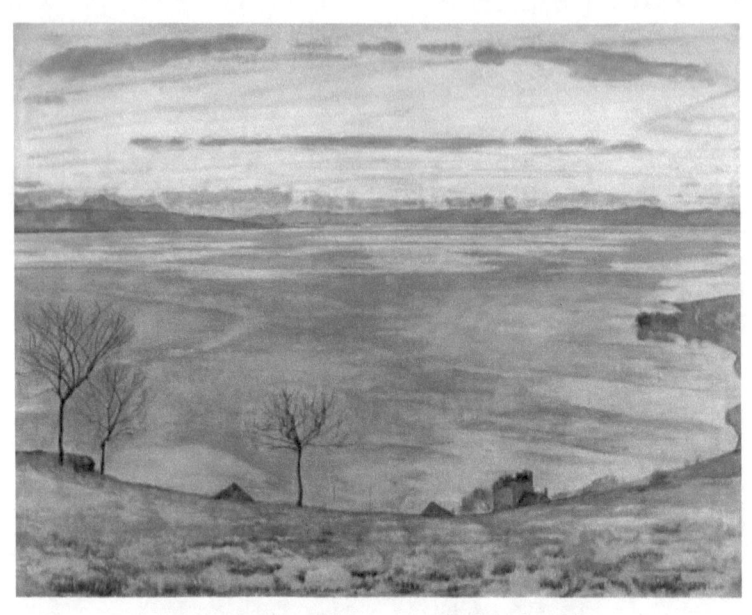

Lake Geneva on the evening in Chexbres
1895, oil on canvas

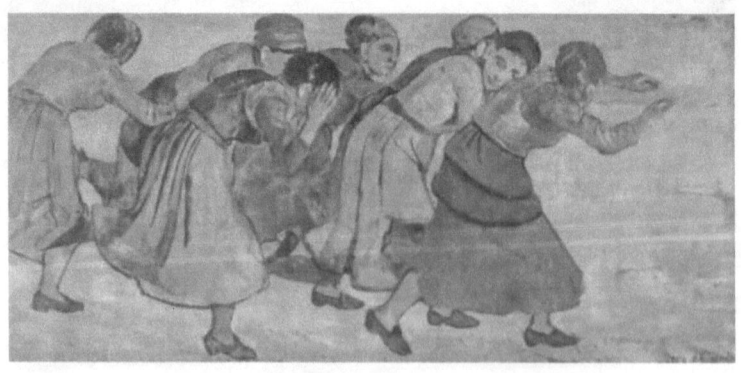

Running women
1895, oil on canvas

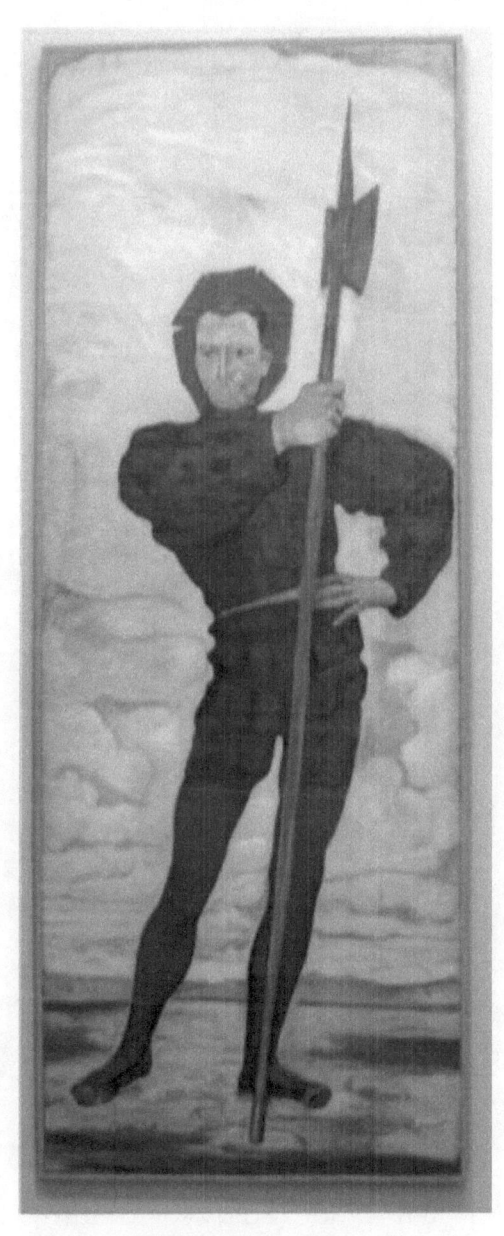

The Halberdier
1895, oil on canvas

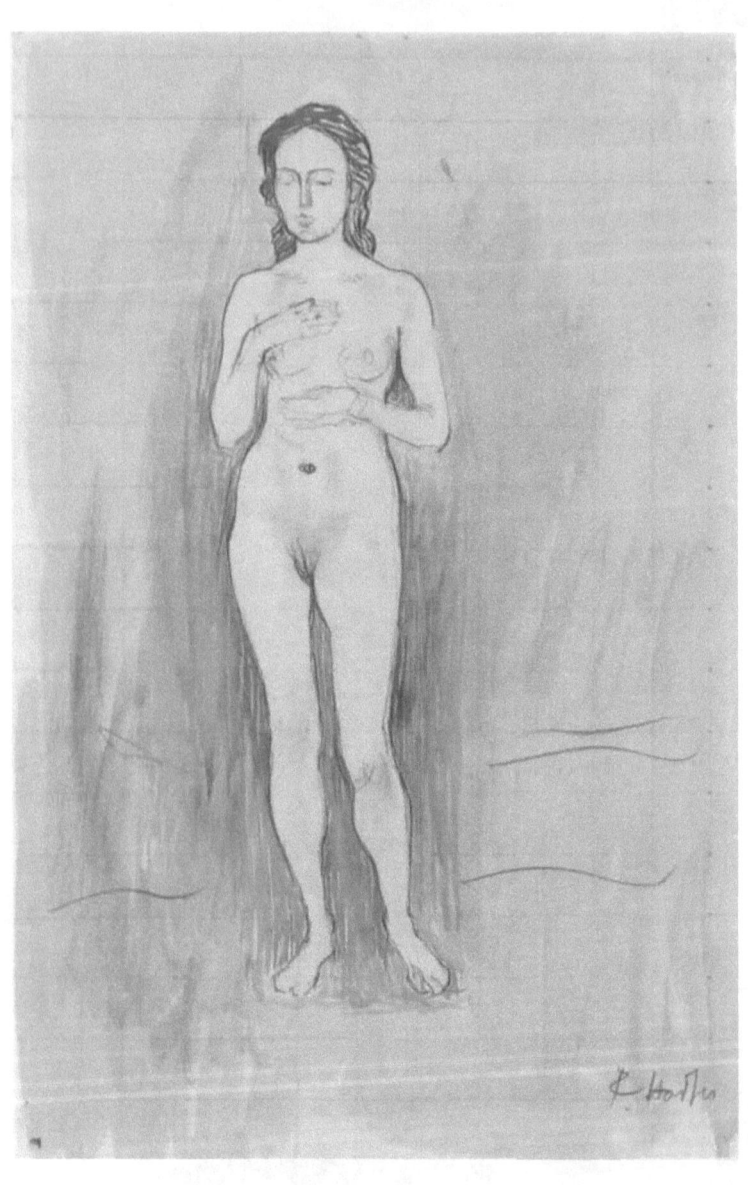

Female Nude (Study for "Truth")
1896, pencil, chalk, watercolor

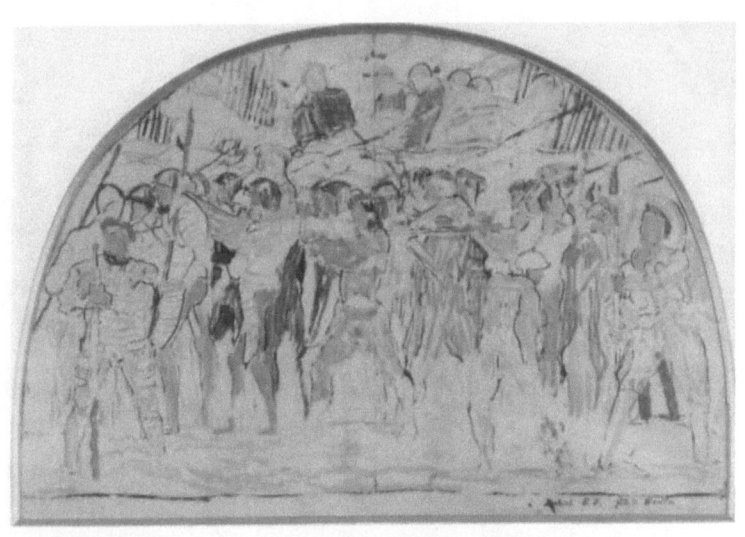

Compositional study to retreat from Marignano
1897, gouache, pencil

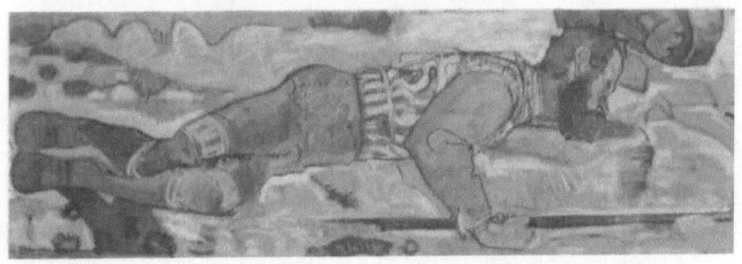

Dying Warrior
1897, oil on canvas

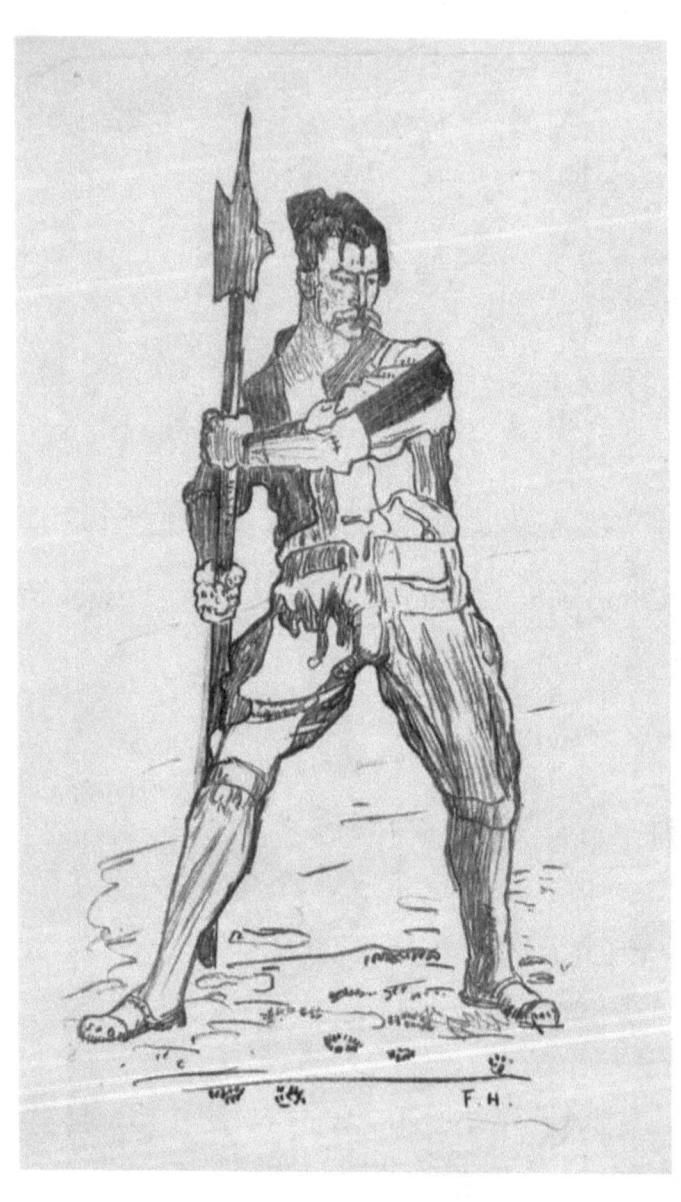

Landsknecht with halberd
1897, pencil

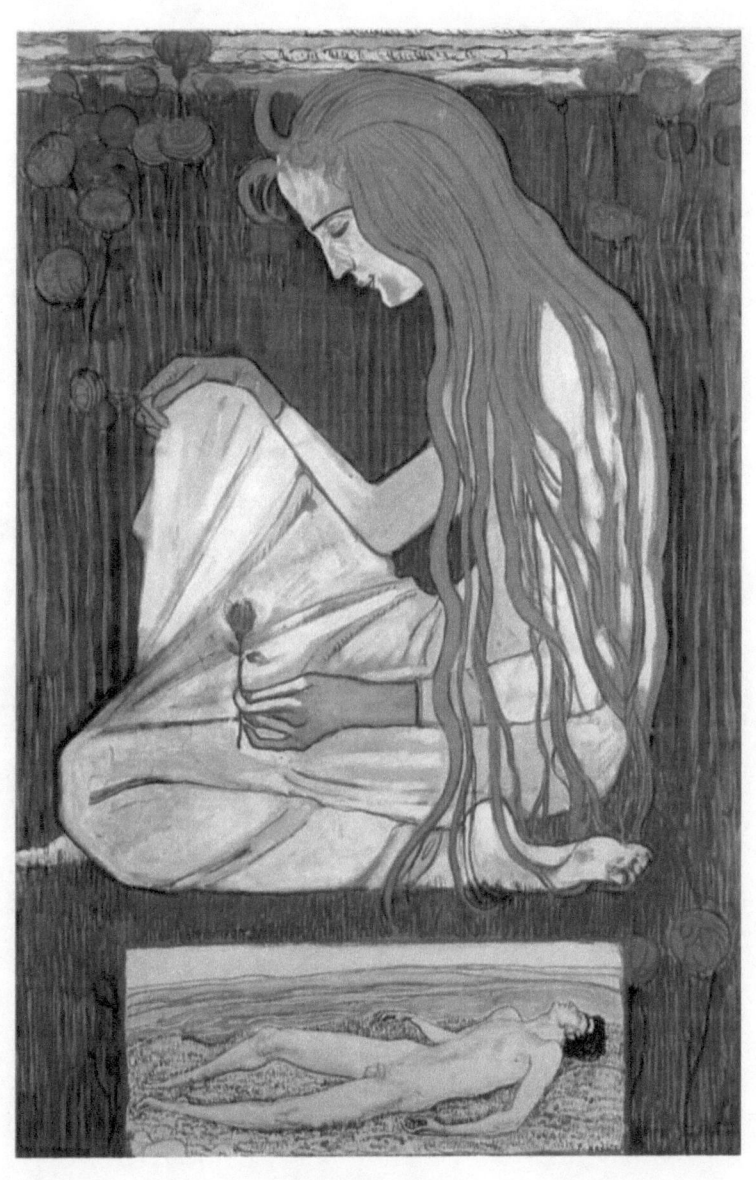

The Dream
1897, watercolor

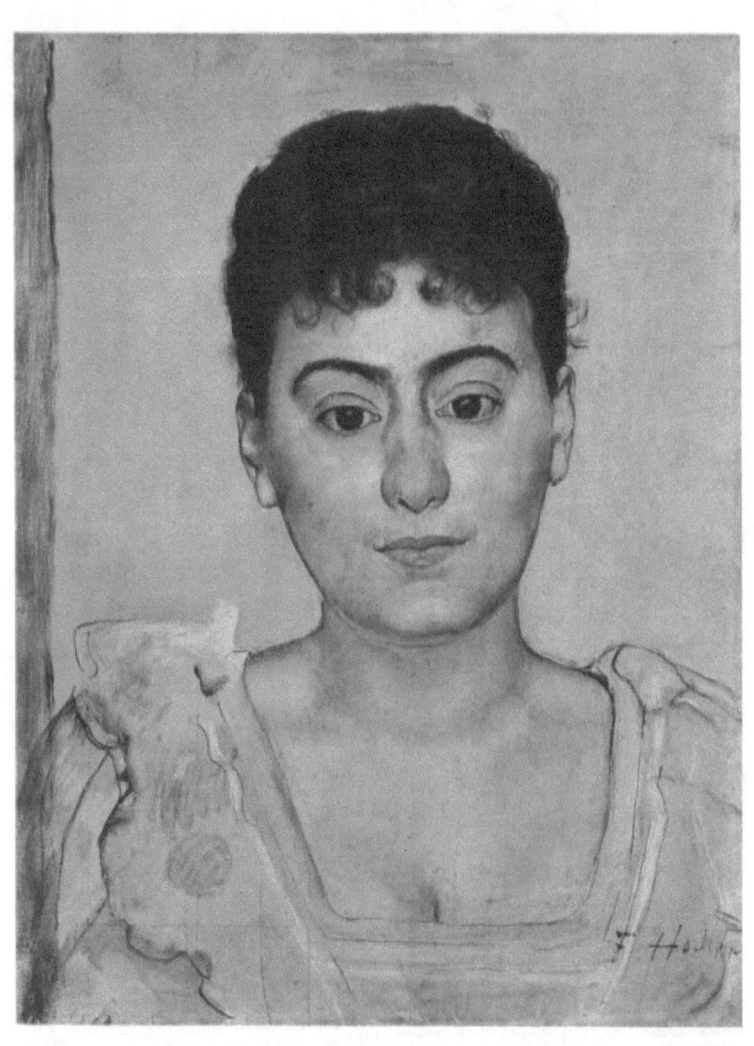

Portrait of Madame de R.
1898, oil on canvas

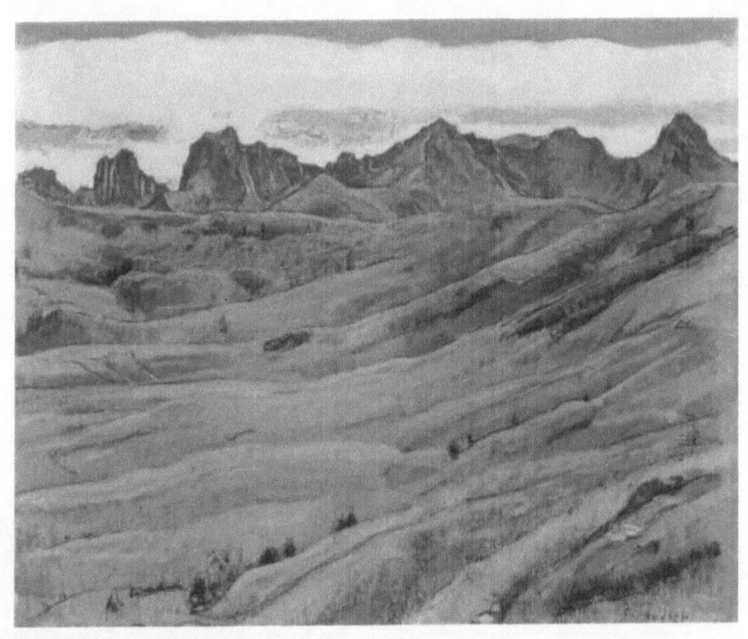

The Gantrisch
1898, oil on canvas

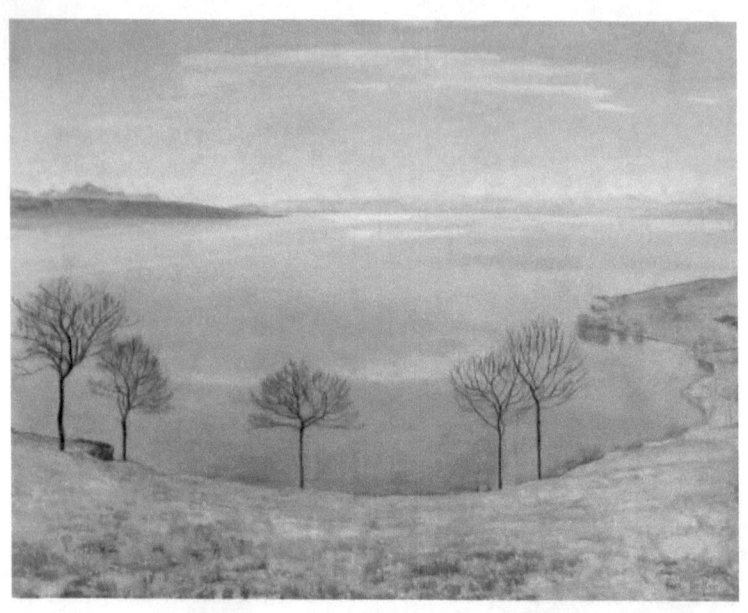

The Lake Geneva from Chexbres
1898, watercolor

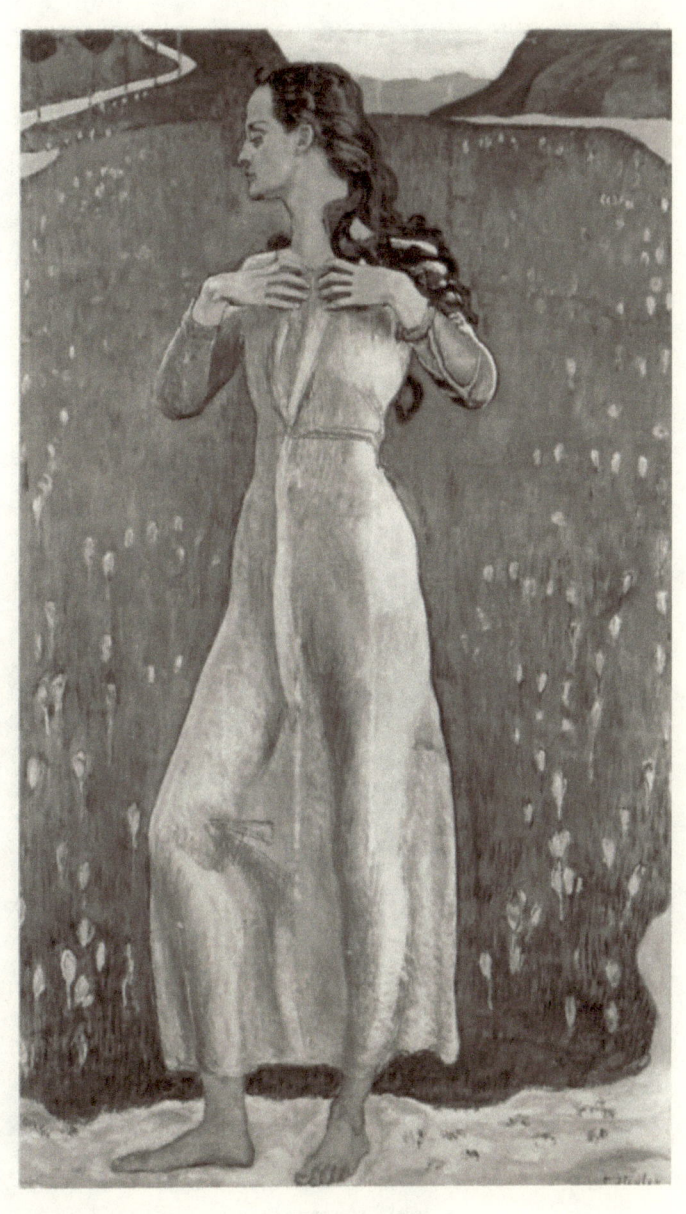

Emotion
1900, oil on canvas

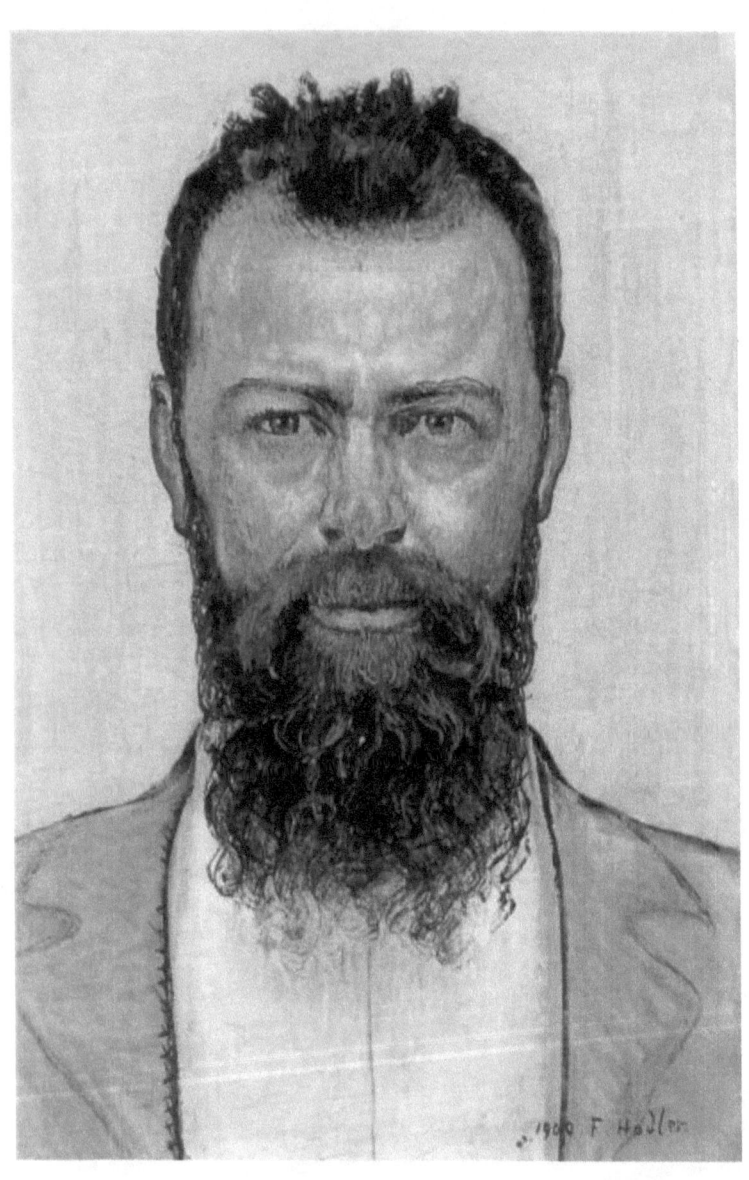

Self-portrait
1900, oil on canvas

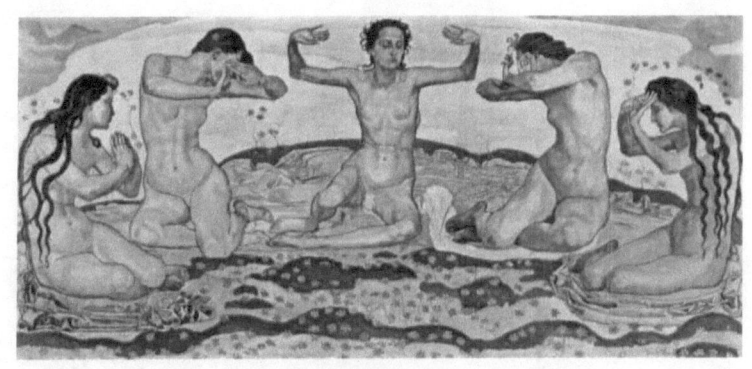

The day
1900, oil on canvas

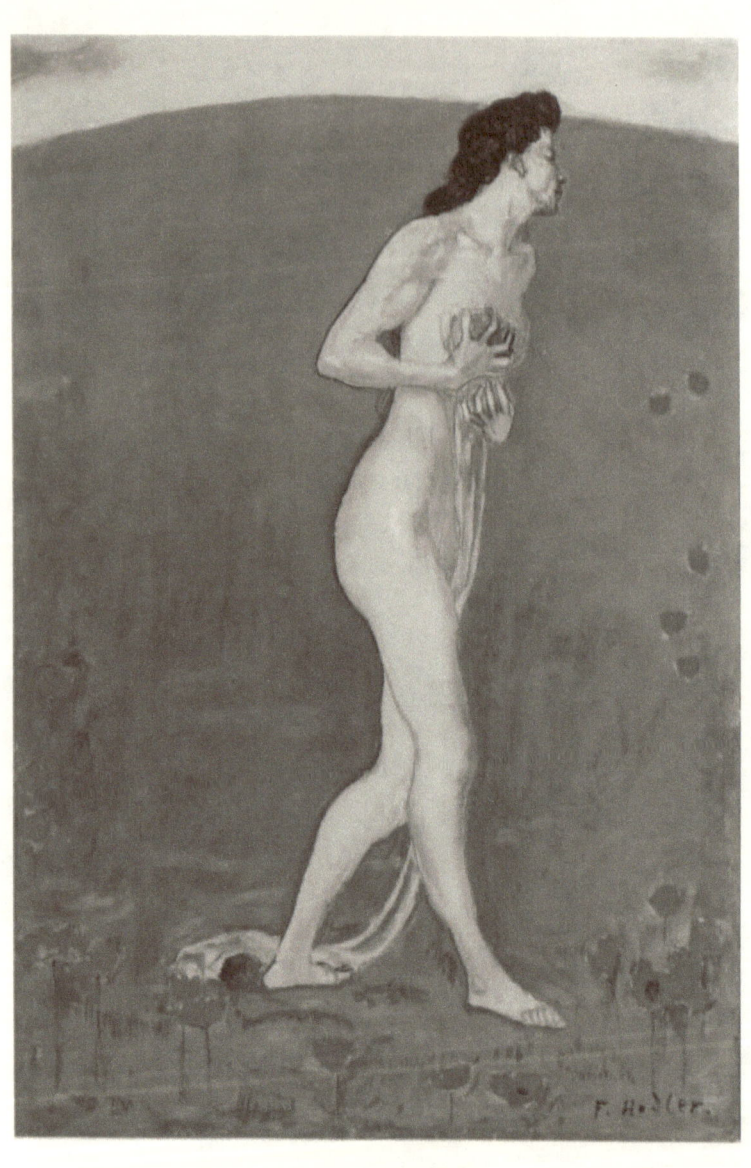

Sensation
1901, oil on canvas

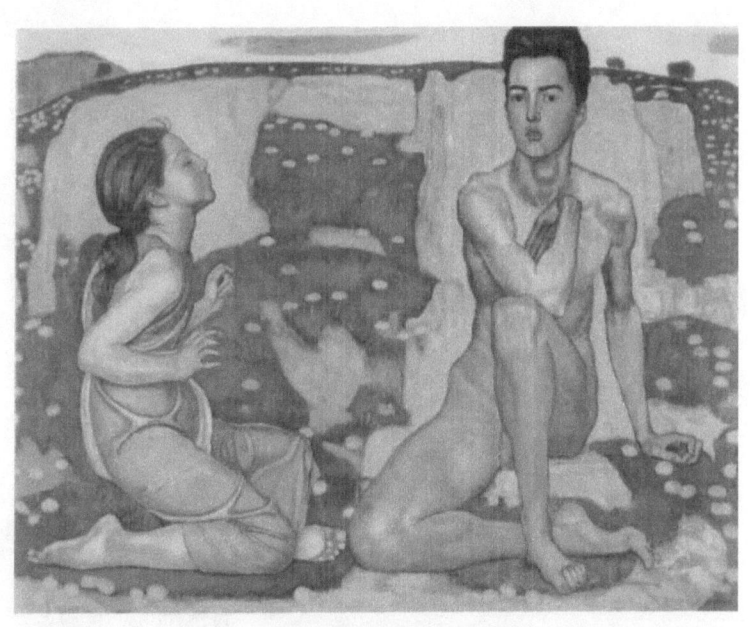

Spring
1901, oil on canvas

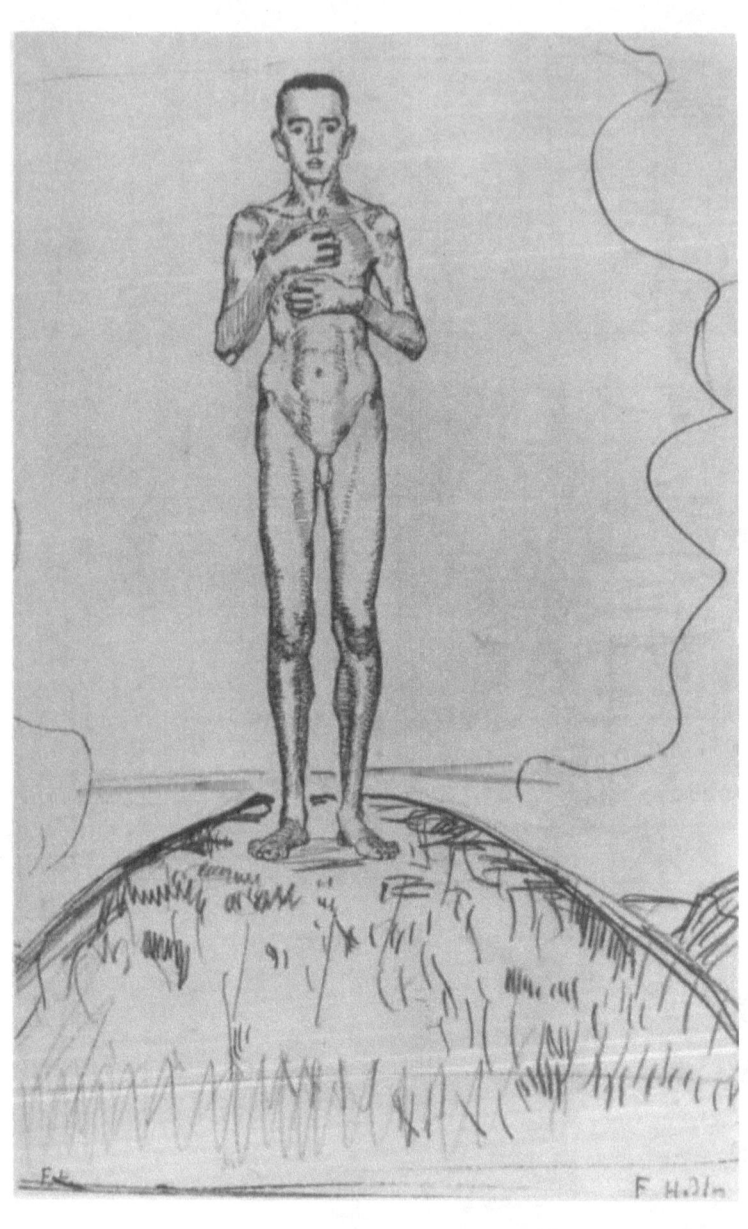

Young Man standing on a hill
1901, pencil

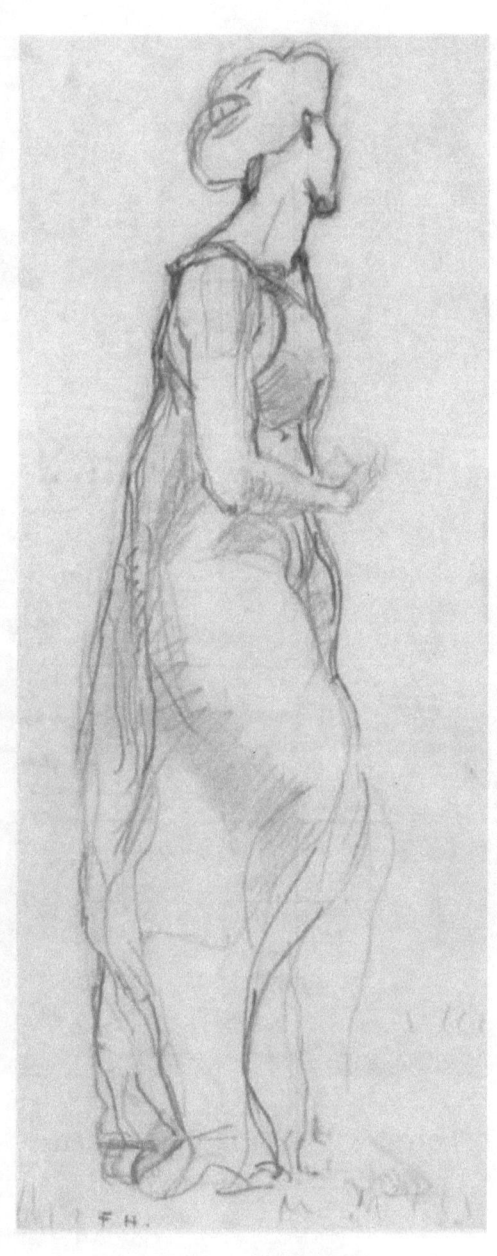

Character study
1902, pencil

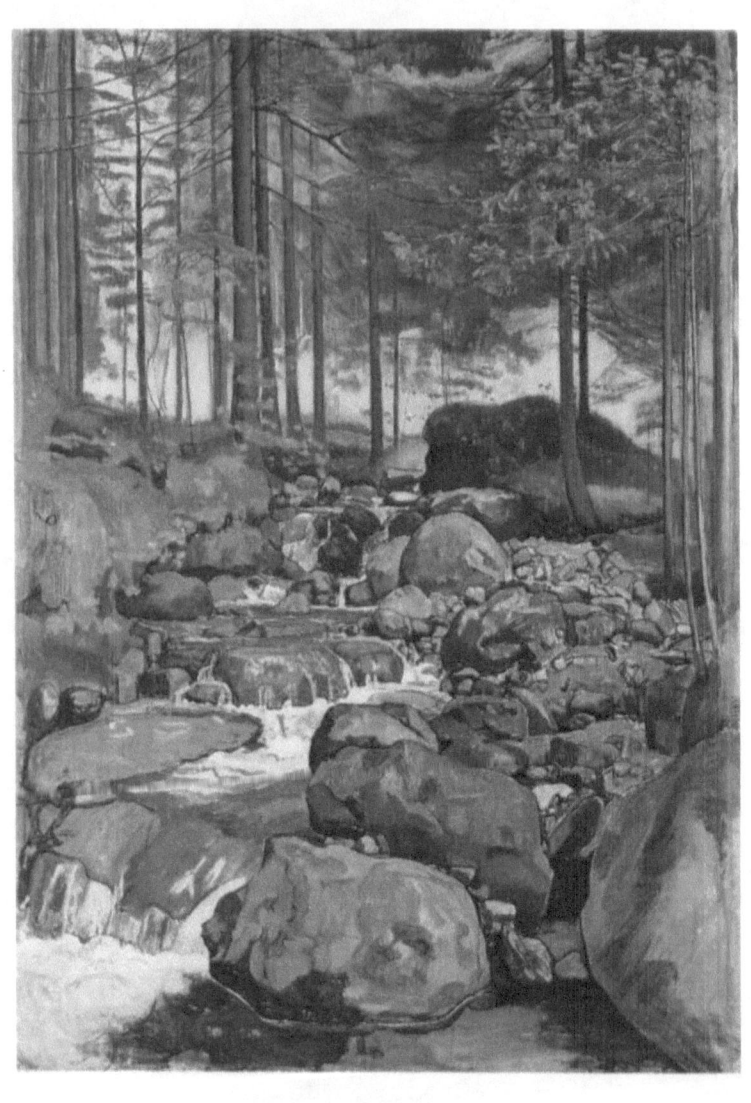

Forest with a mountain stream
1902, oil on canvas

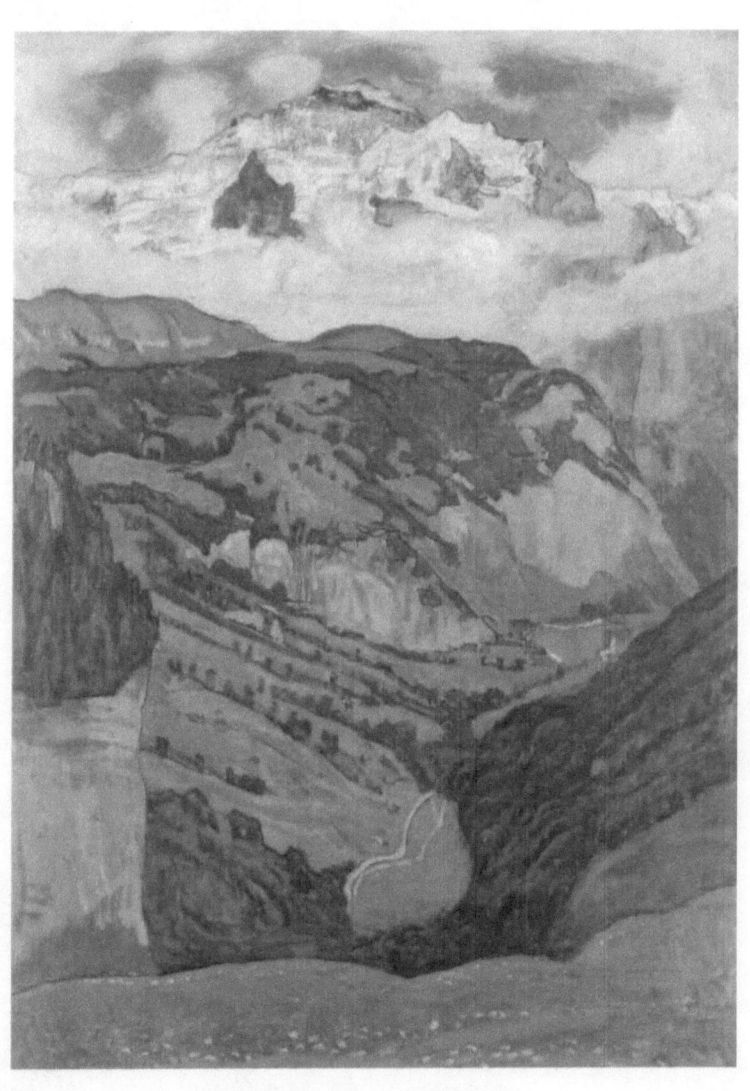

The Lady of the Isenfluh
1902, oil on canvas

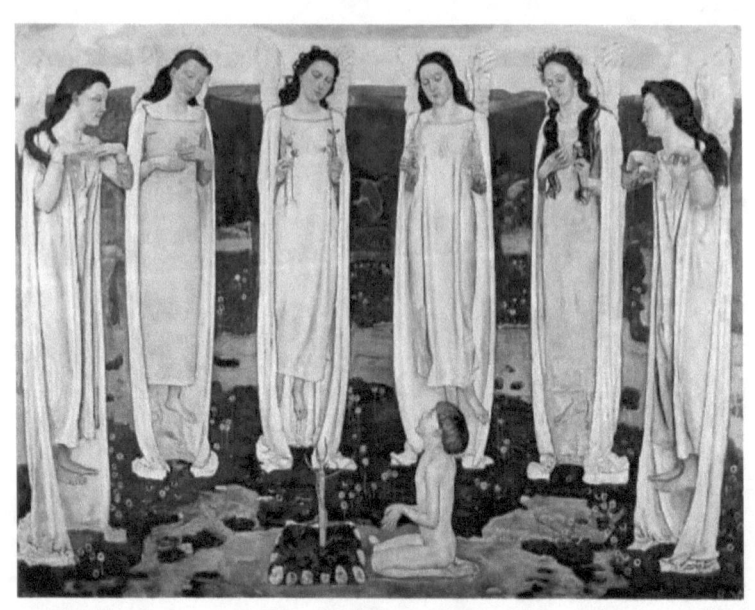

The Consecrated One 1
1903, oil on canvas

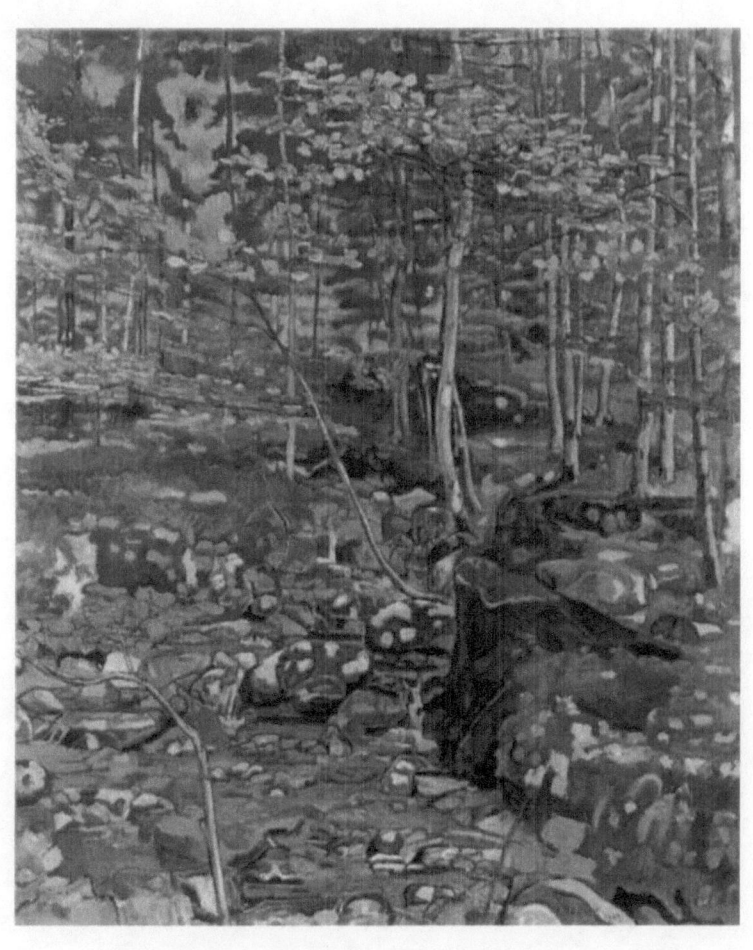

The Forest near Reichenbach
1903, oil on canvas

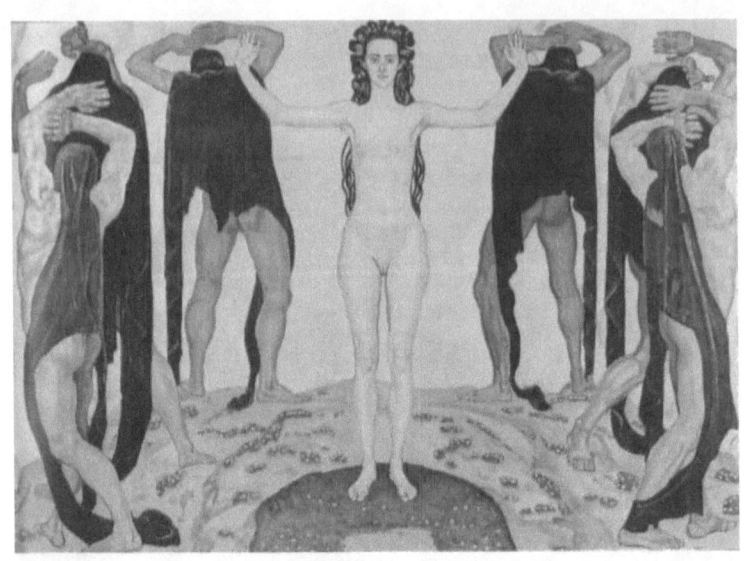

The truth
1903, oil on canvas

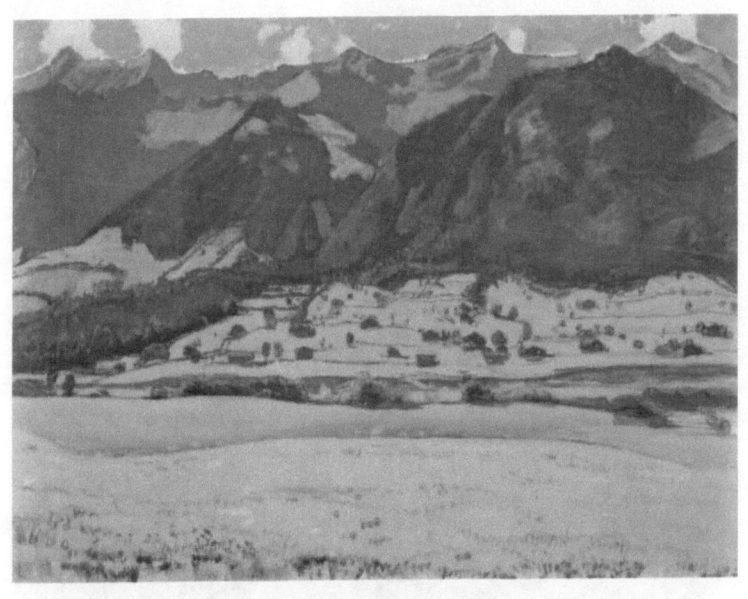

View of the Horn of Fromberg from Reichenbach
1903, oil on canvas

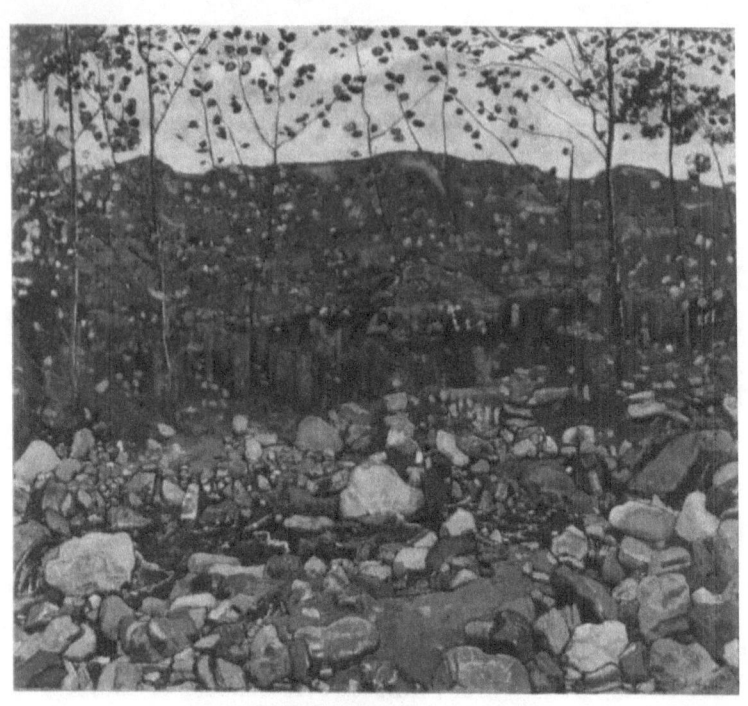

Forest Brook at Leissingen
1904, oil on canvas

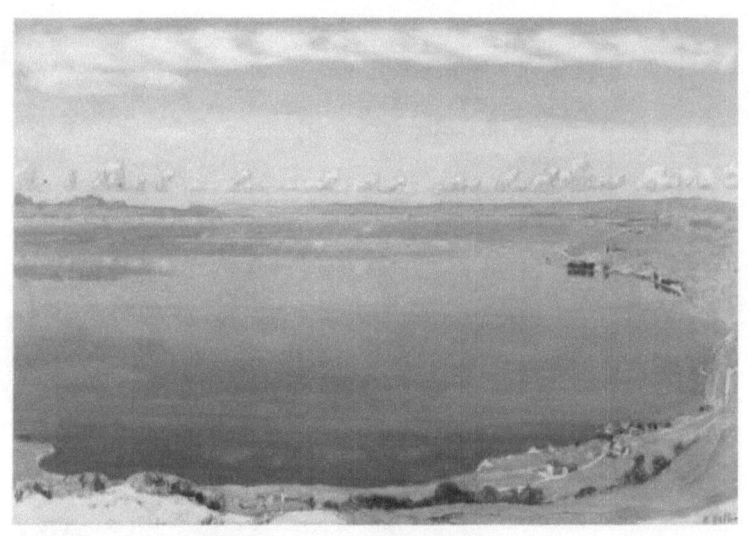

Lake Geneva from Chexbres
1904, oil on canvas

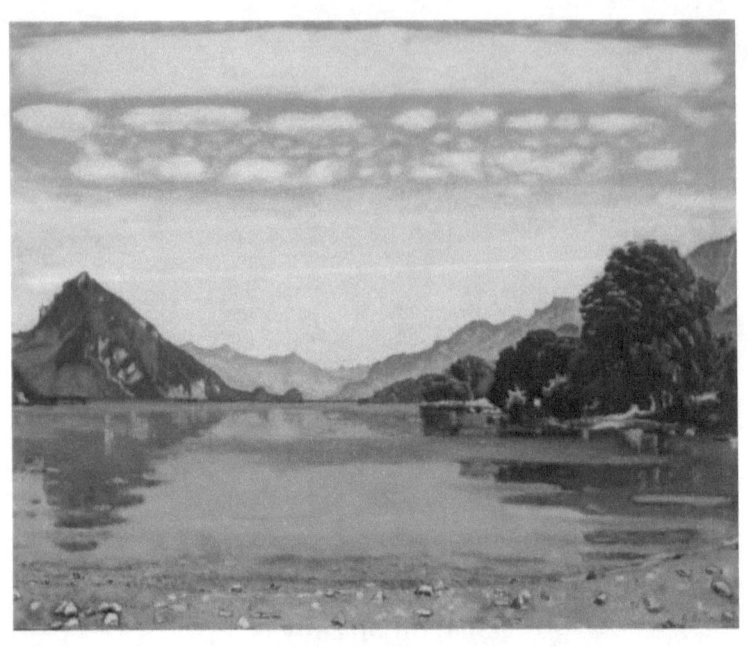

Lake Thun from Lessig
1904, oil on canvas

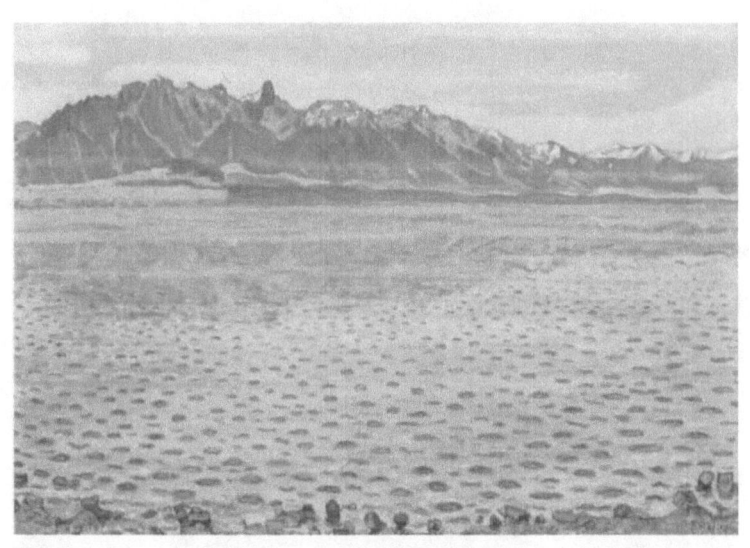

Thun, Stockhornkette
1904, oil on canvas

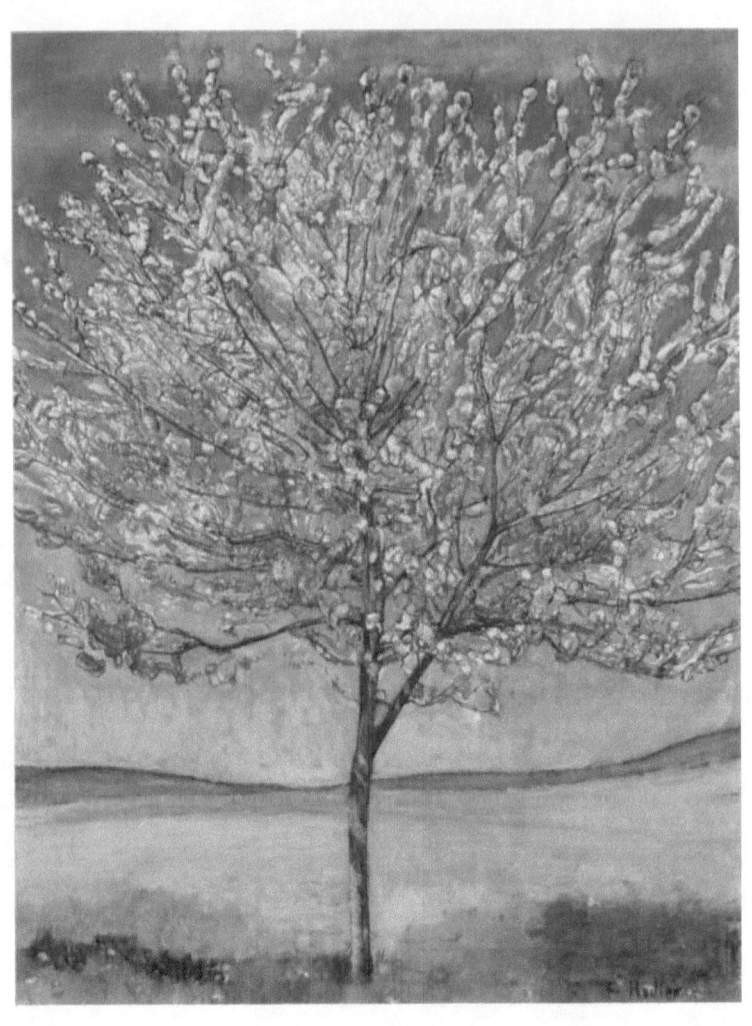

Cherry Tree in Bloom
1905, oil on canvas

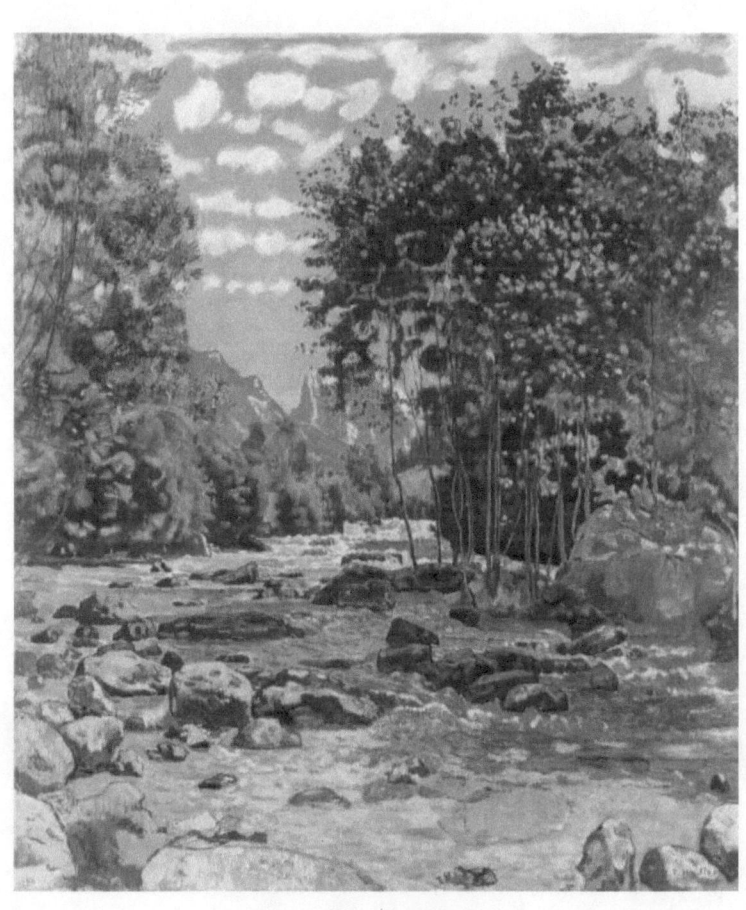

The Black Lutschina
1905, oil on canvas

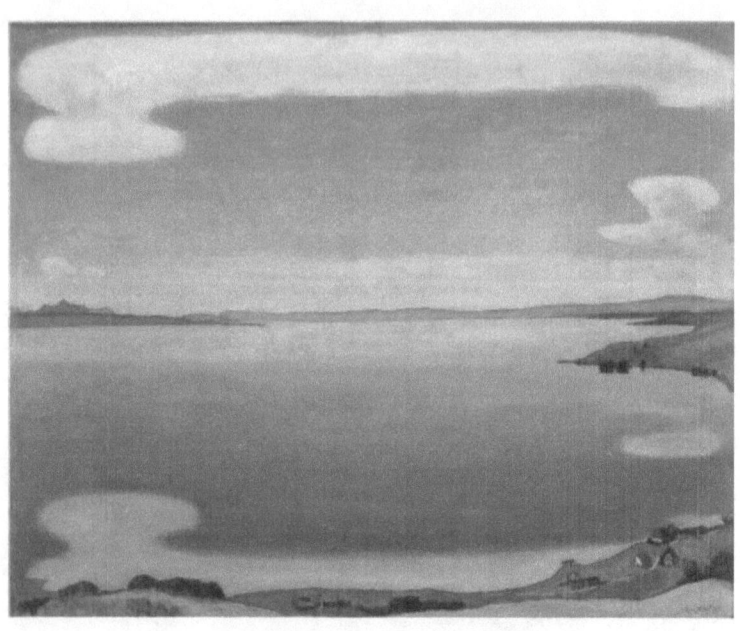

Lake Geneva from Chexbres
1905, oil on canvas

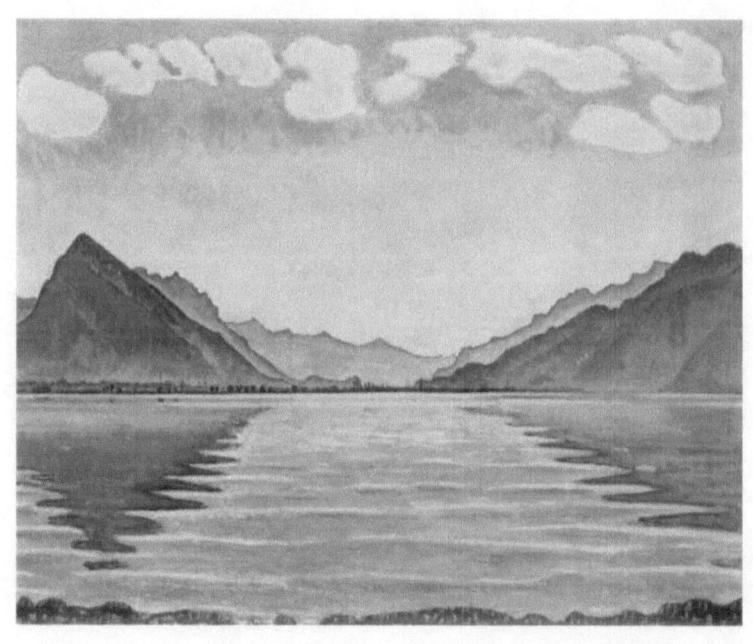

Lake Thun, Symmetric reflection
1905, oil on canvas

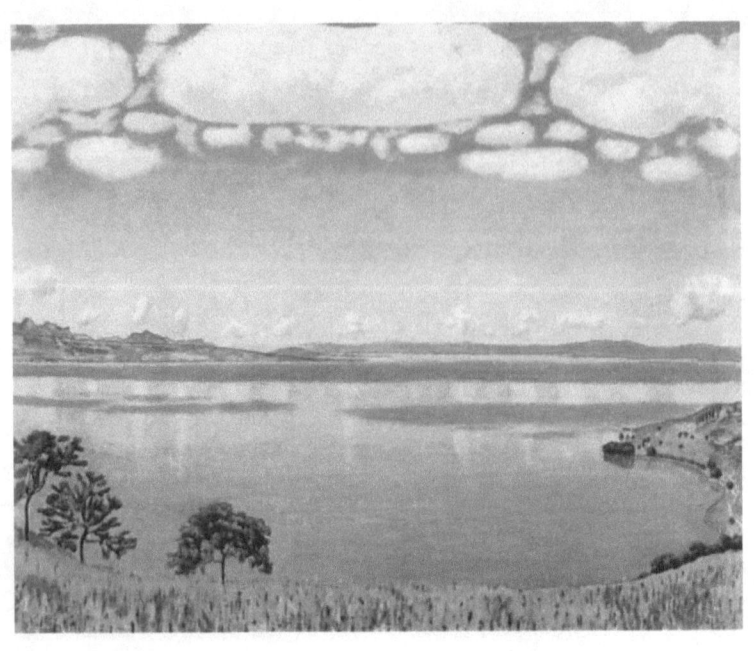

View of Lake Leman from Chexbres
1905, oil on canvas

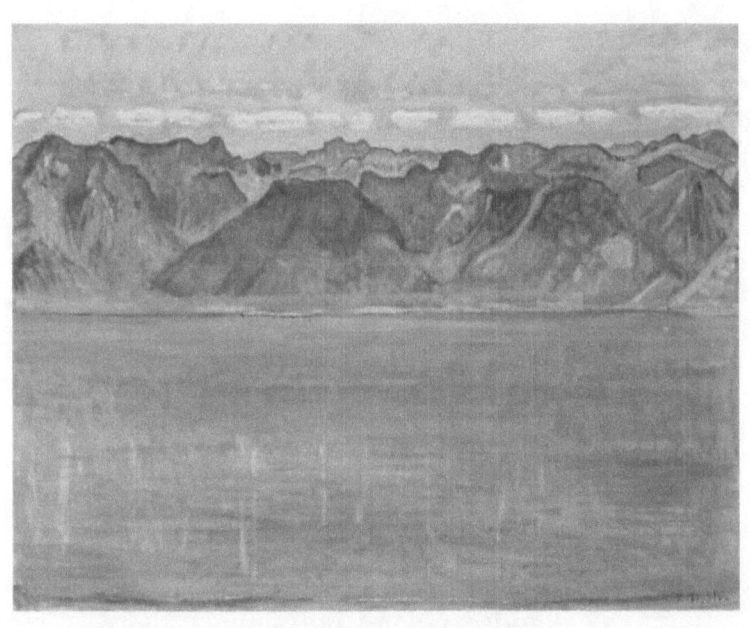

Lake Geneva, overlooking the Savoyerberge
1906, oil on canvas

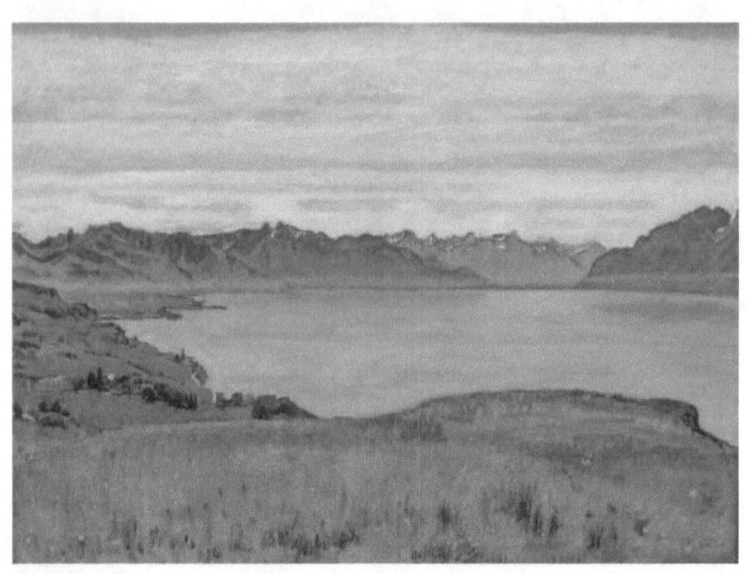

Landscape on Lake Geneva
1906, oil on canvas

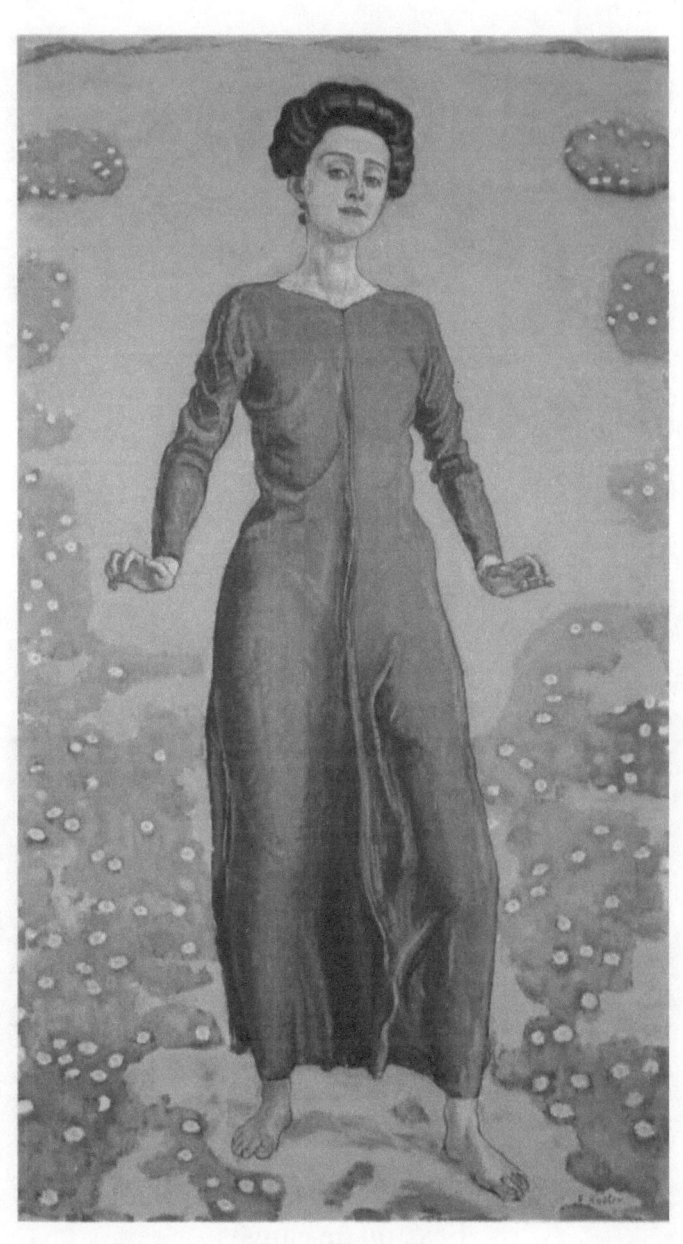

Transfiguration
1906, oil on canvas

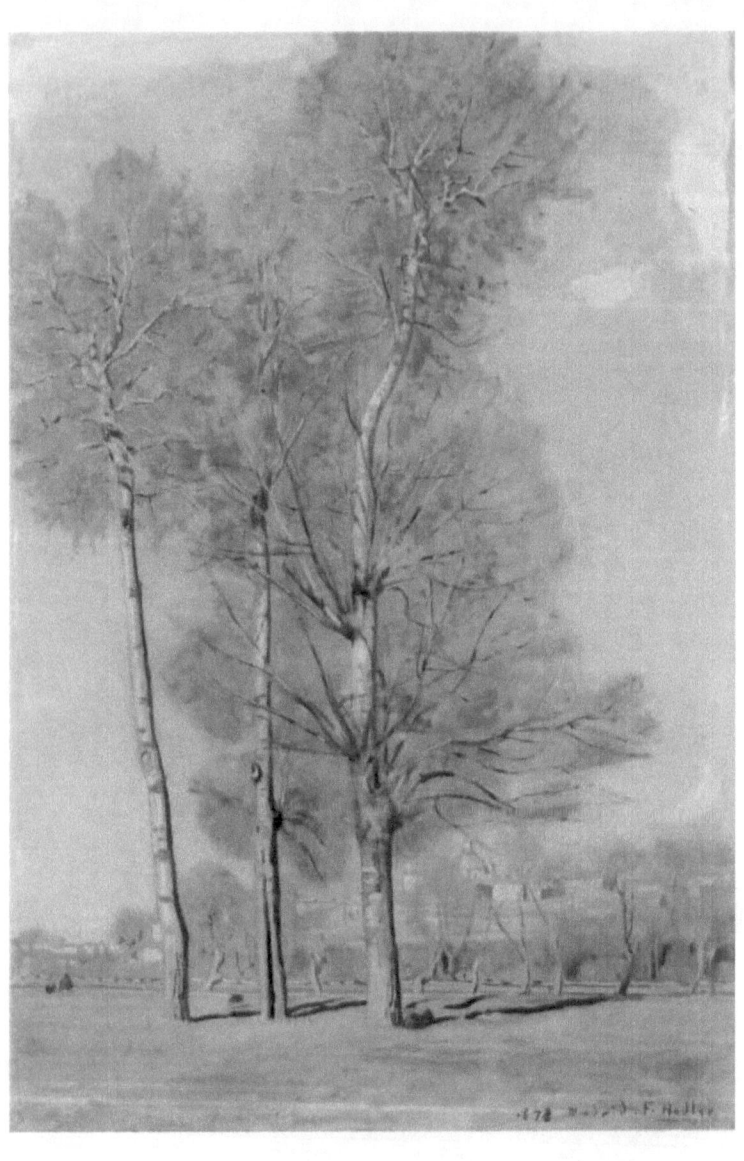

Tree on the Lake of Brienz near Bödeli
1906, oil on canvas

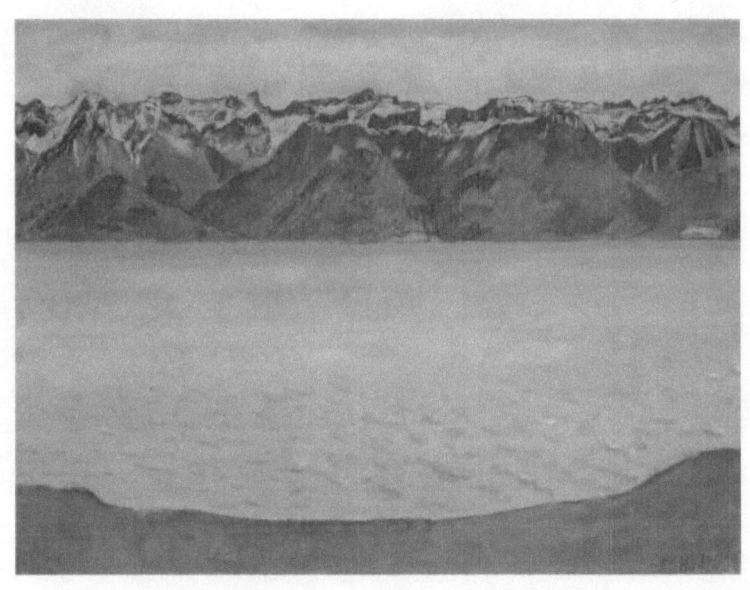

Lake Geneva with Savoyerbergen
1907, oil on canvas

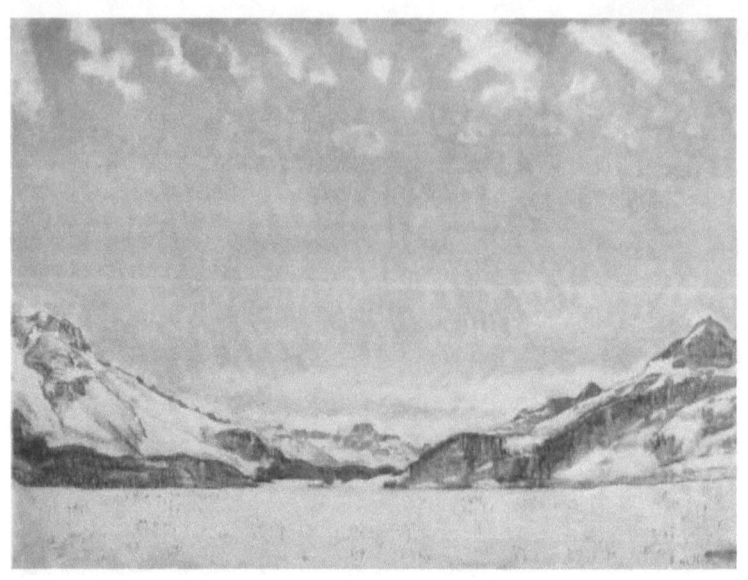

Snow in the Engadine
1907, oil on canvas

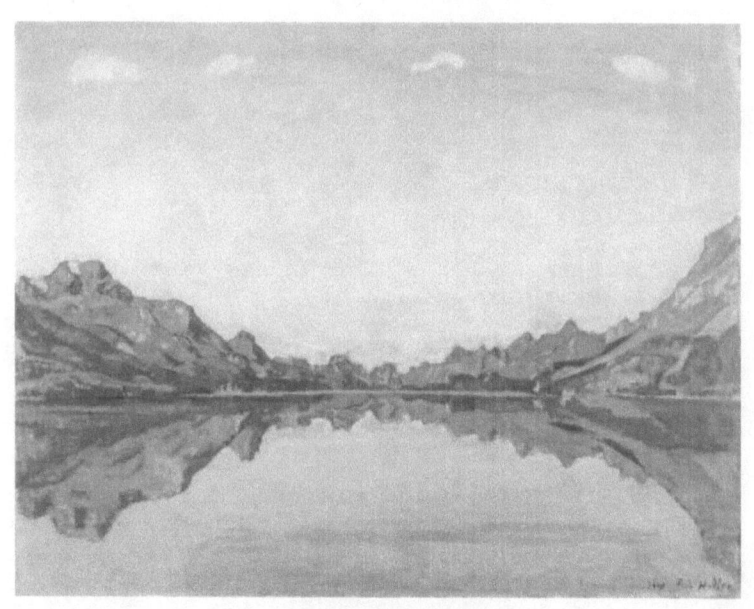

The fall in Silvaplana
1907, oil on canvas

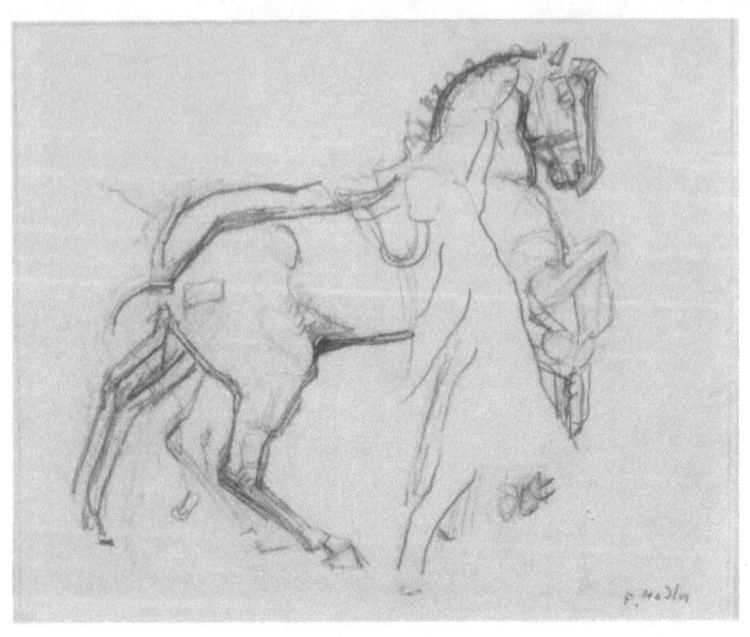

Cavalryman striding a horse
1908, pencil

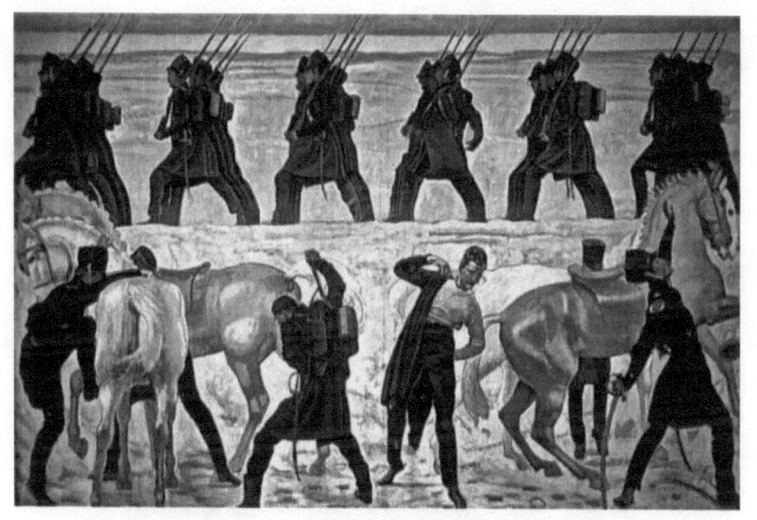

Jena Students Depart for the War of Liberation
1908, oil on canvas

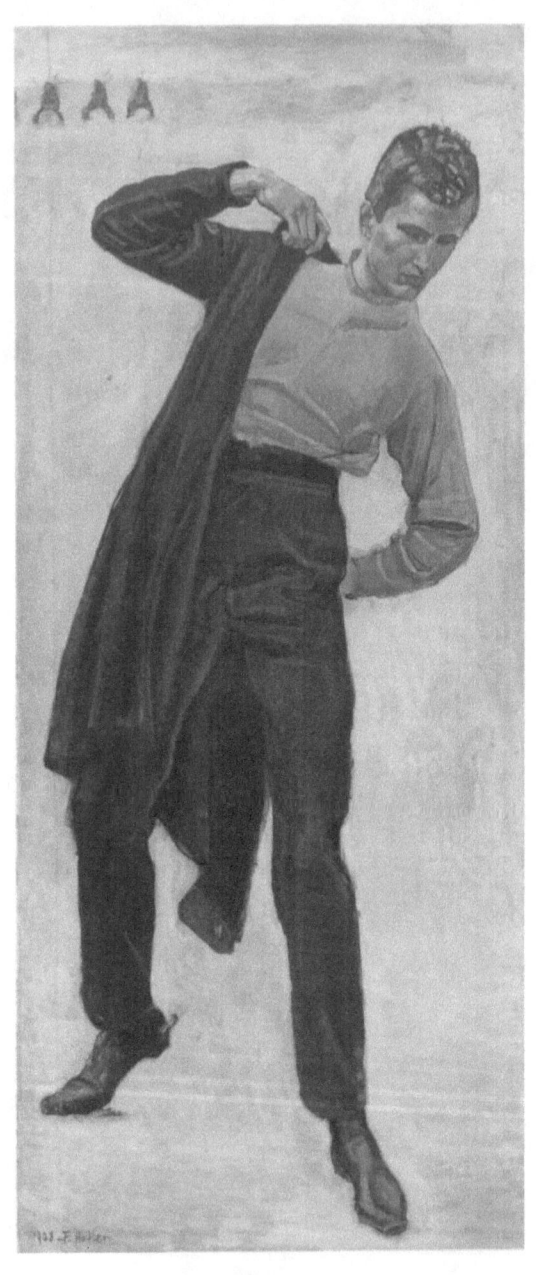

Jenenser Student
1908, oil on canvas

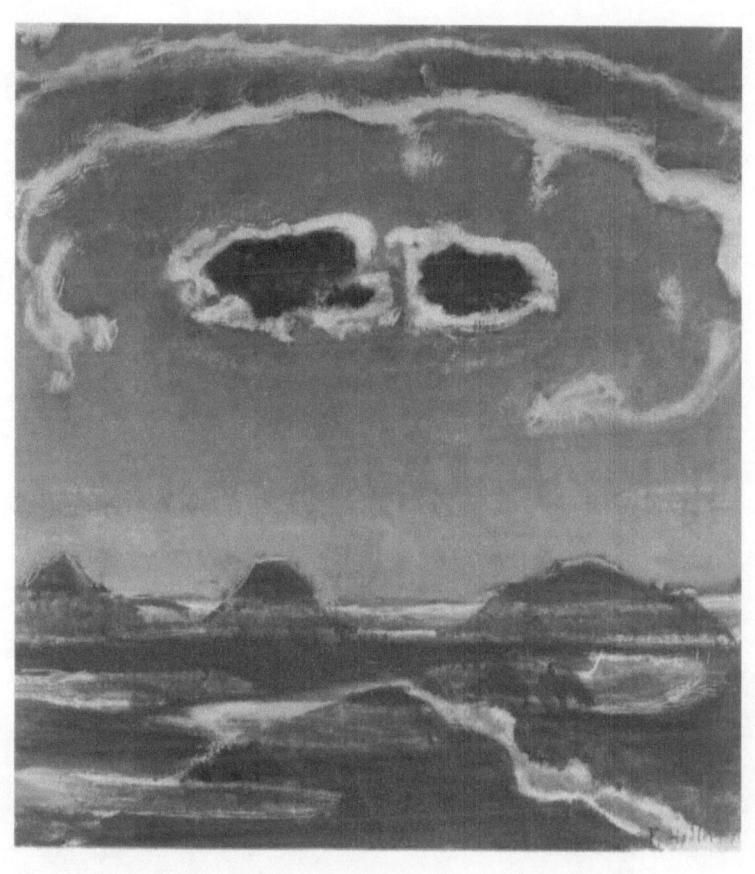

Eiger, Monch and Jungfrau in Moonlight
1908, oil on canvas

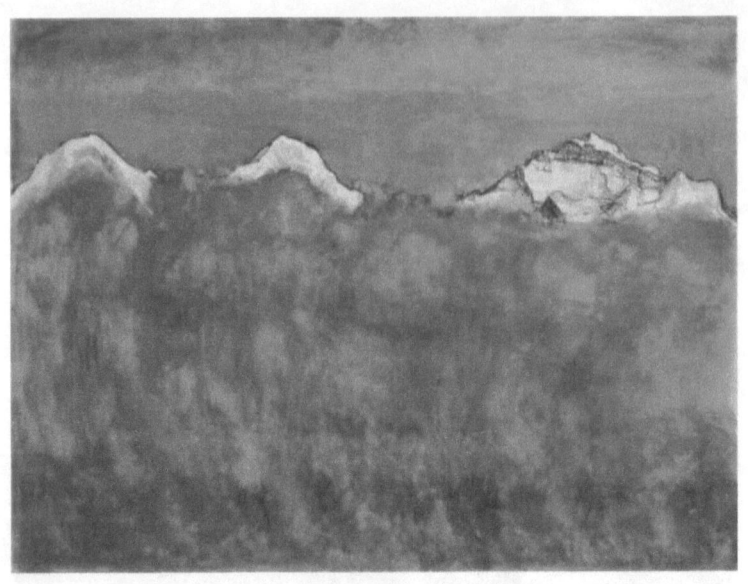

Eiger, Monch and Jungfrau in Moonlight
1908, oil on canvas

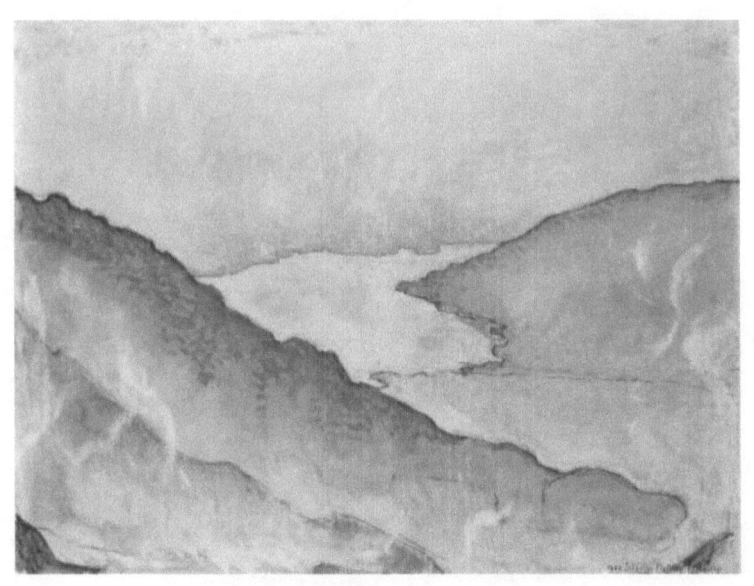

Evening mist on Lake Thun
1908, oil on canvas

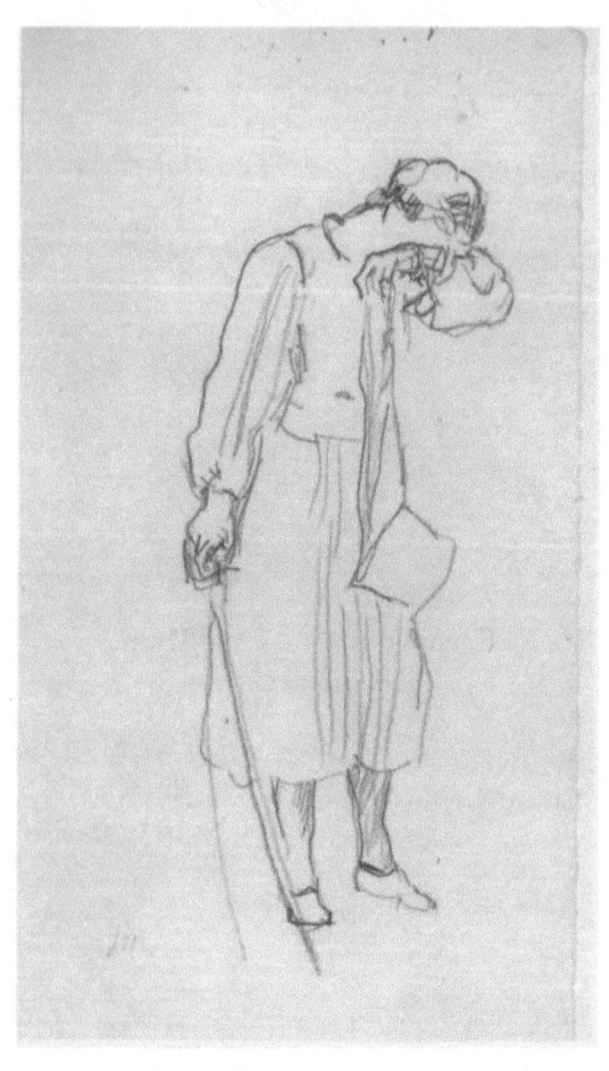

Farewell participating female figure
1908, pencil

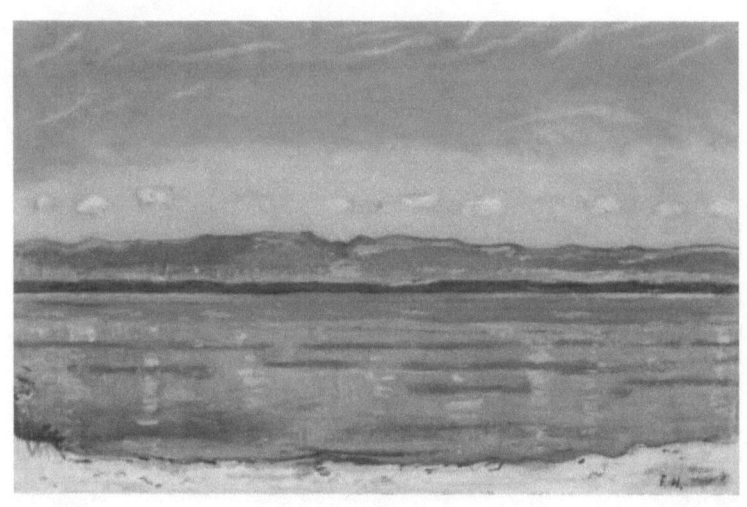

Landscape with of rhythm
1908, oil on canvas

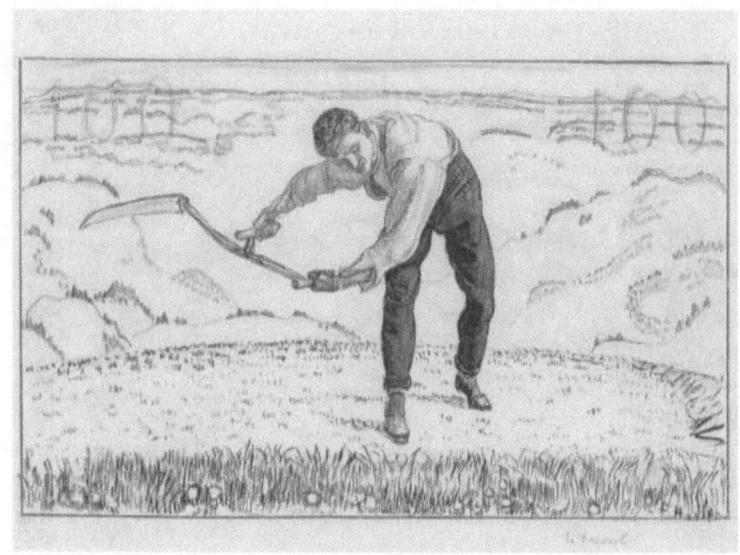

The working mower
1909, pencil, ink

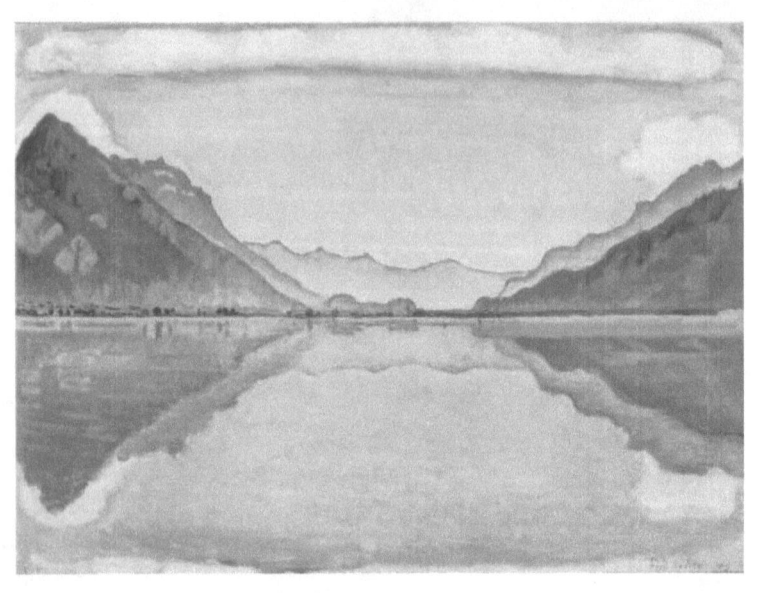

Thun with symmetric mirroring
1909, oil on canvas

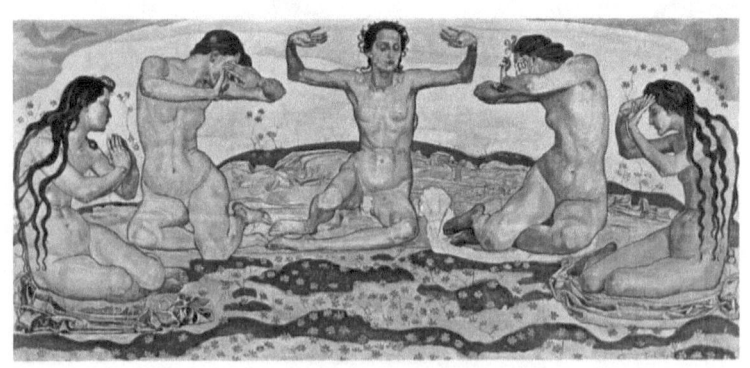

A day
1909, oil on canvas

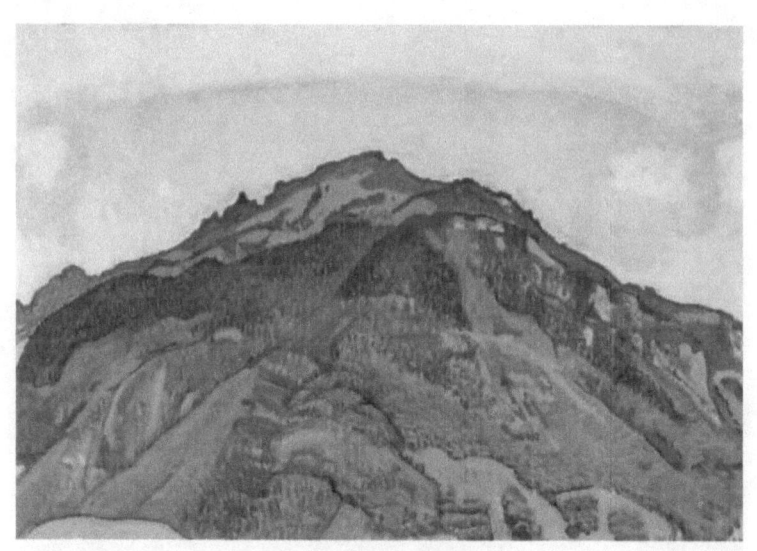

Schynige plate
1909, oil on canvas

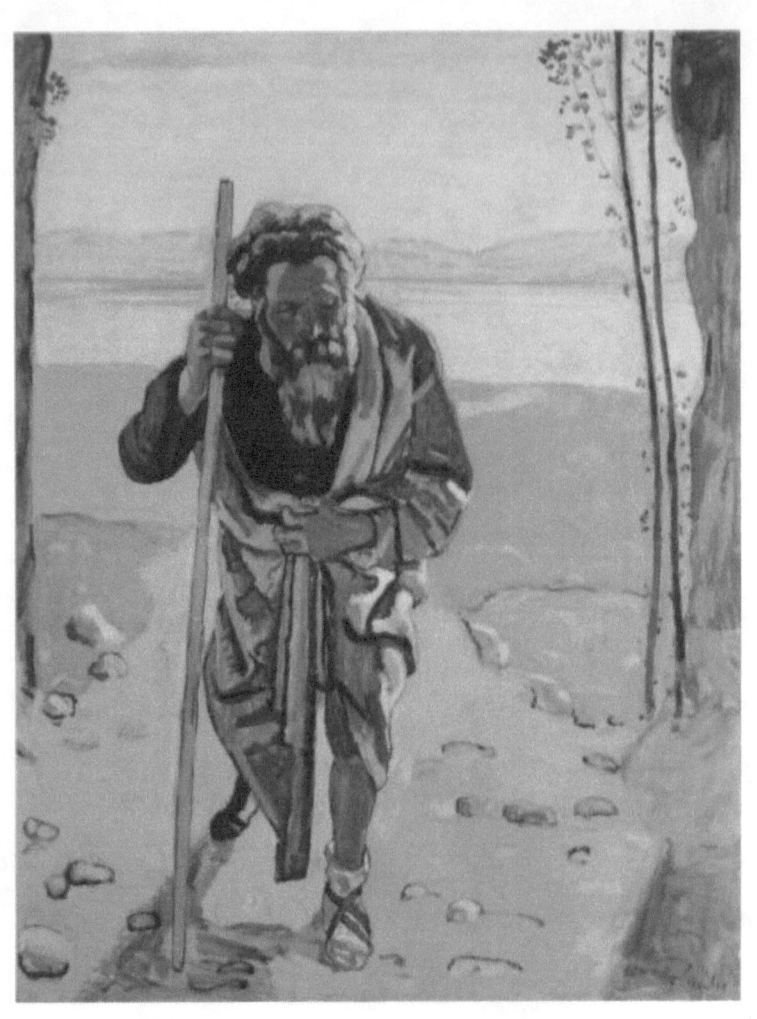

Ahasver
1910, oil on canvas

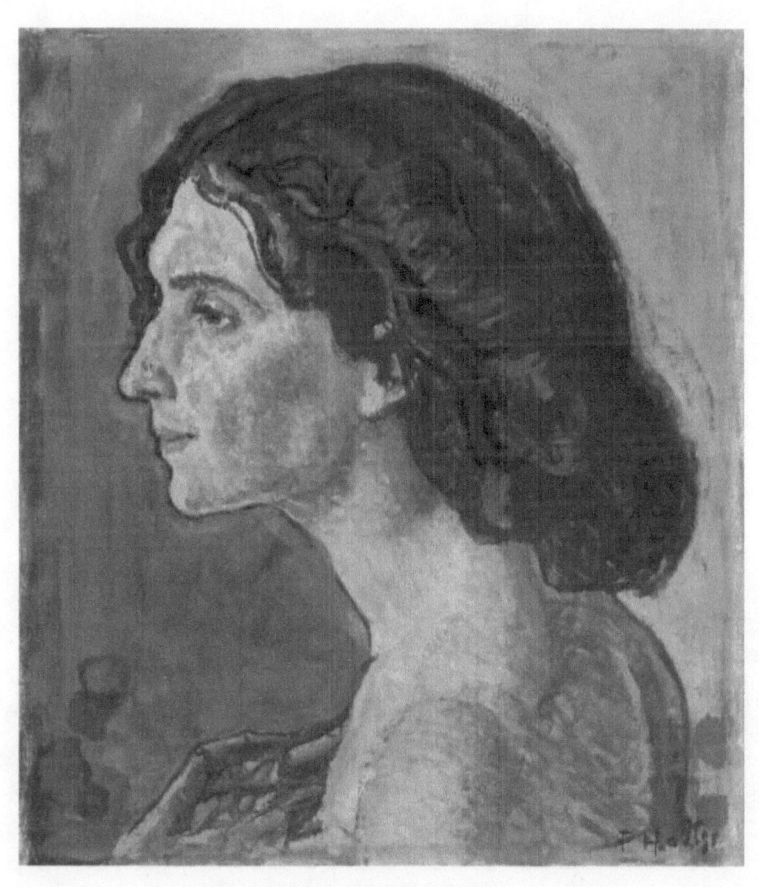

Giulia Leonardi
1910, oil on canvas

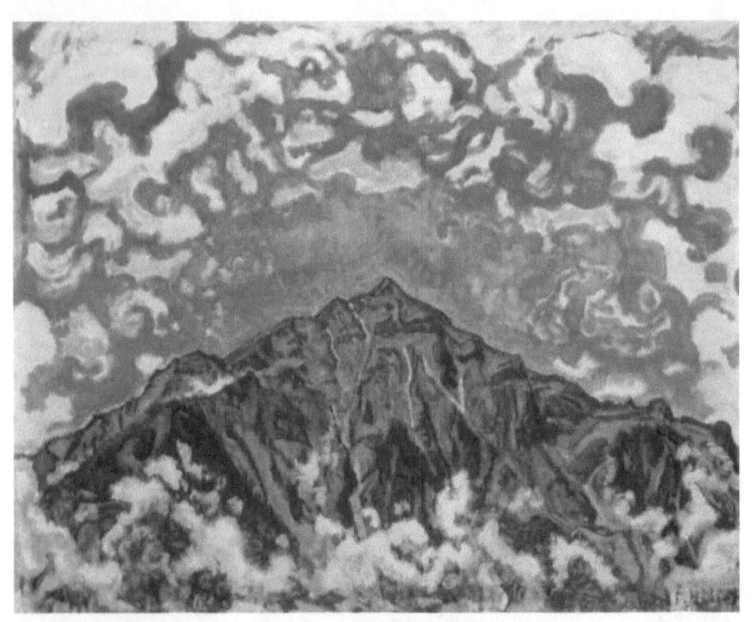

Niesen
1910, oil on canvas

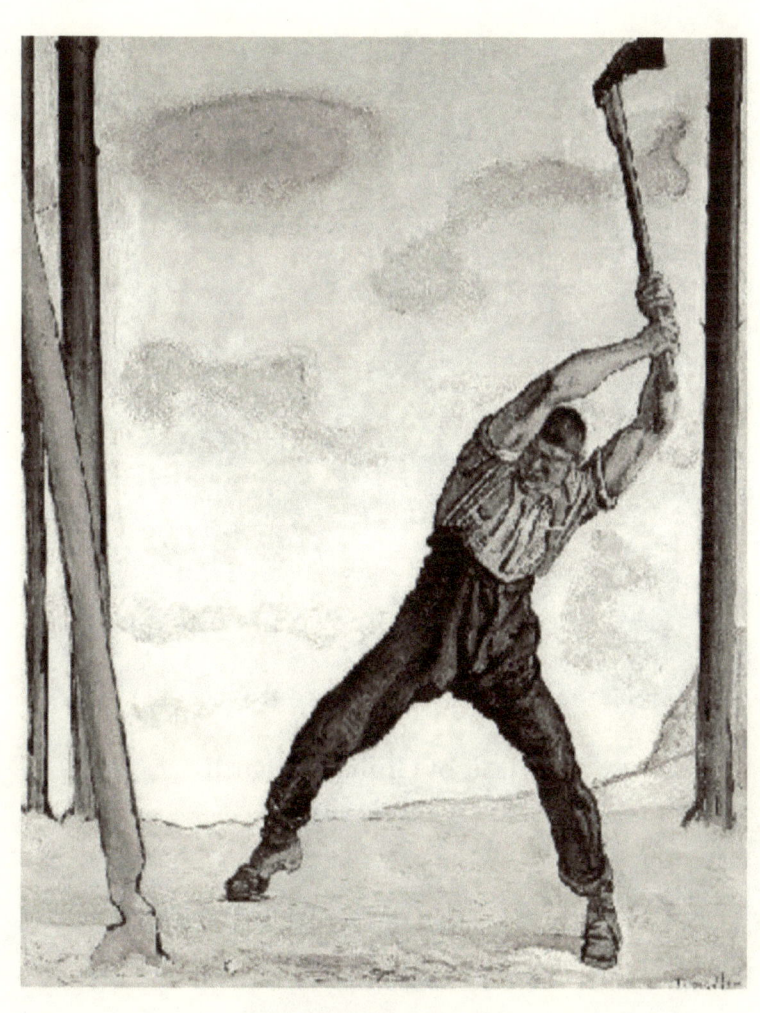

Lumberjack
1910, oil on canvas

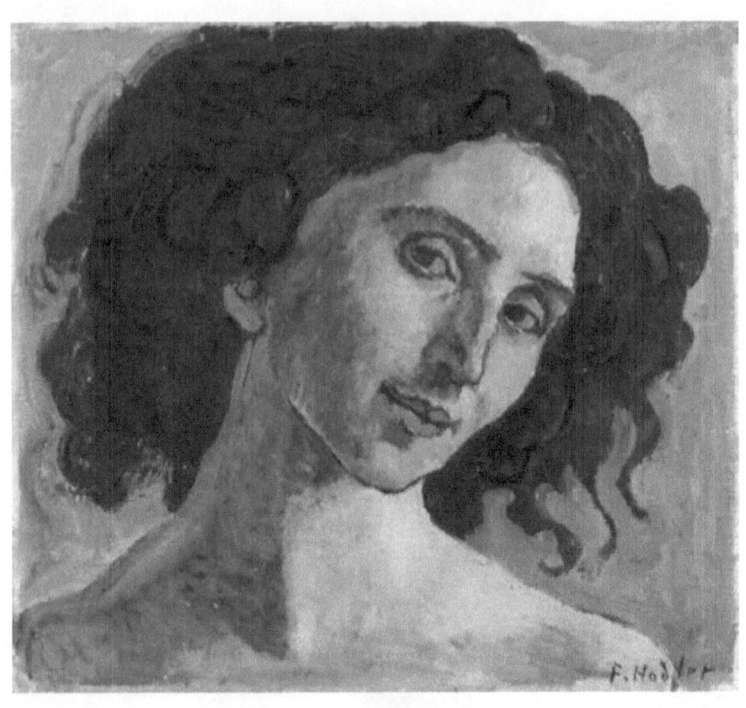

Portrait of Giulia Leonardi
1910, oil on canvas

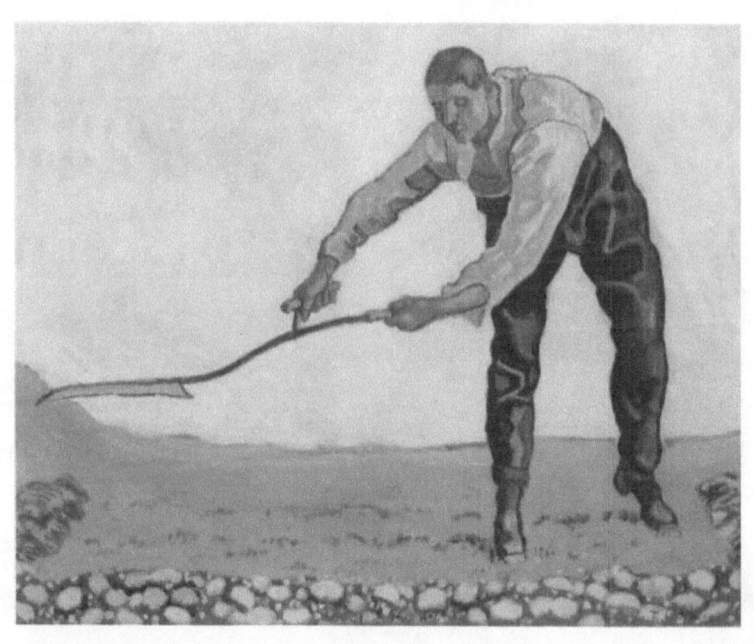

The Reaper
1910, oil on canvas

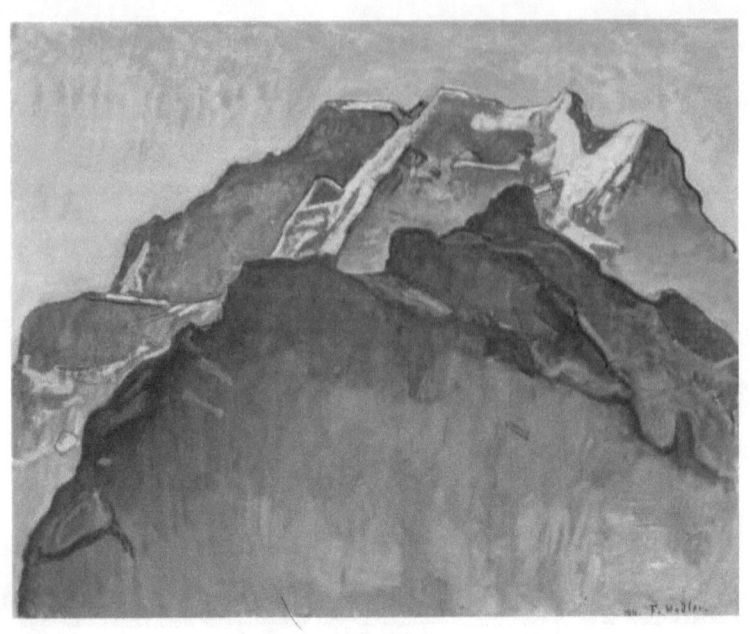

Jungfrau massif and Schwarzmonch
1911, oil on canvas

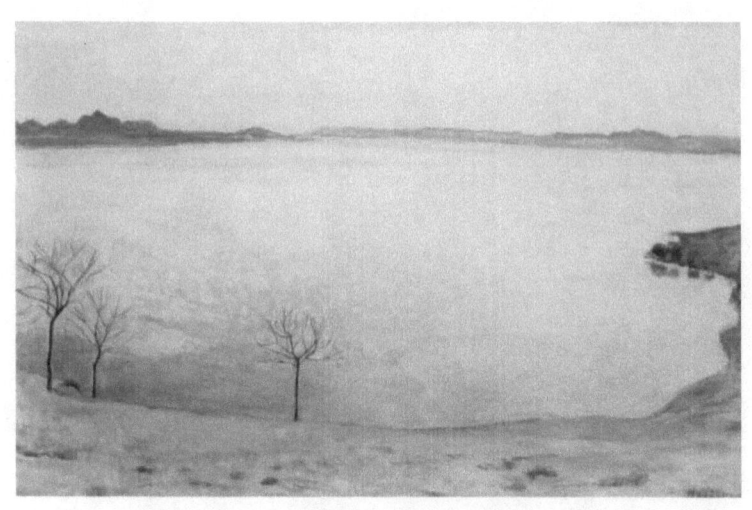

Lake Geneva in Chexbres
1911, oil on canvas

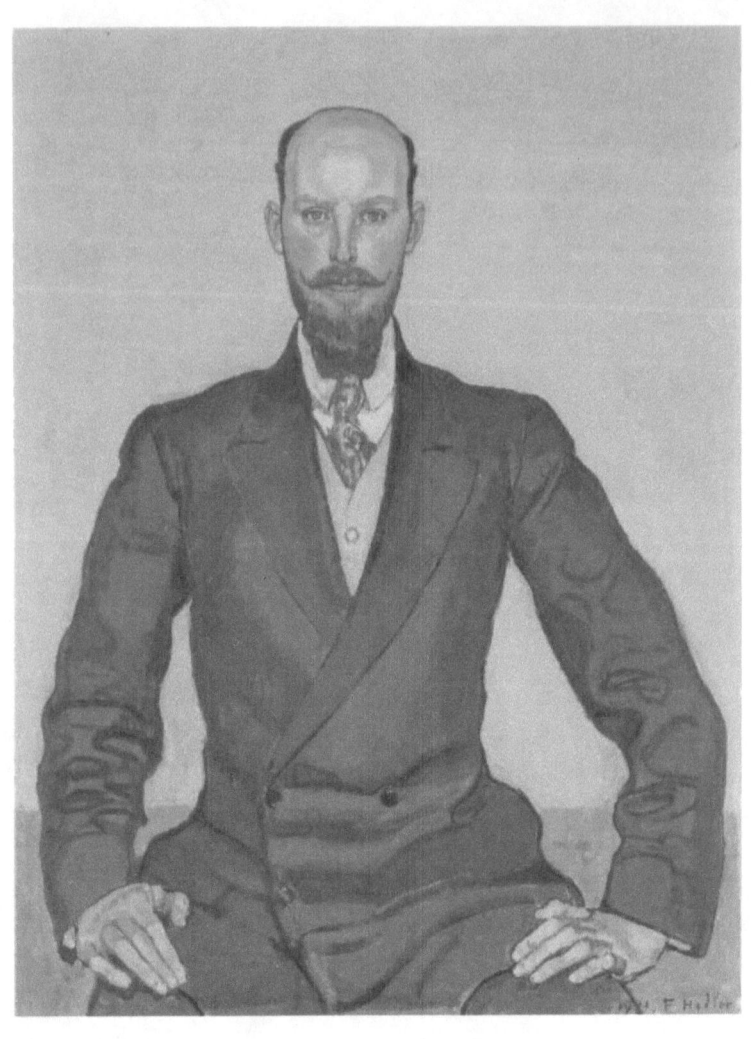

Portrait of Willy Russ
1911, oil on canvas

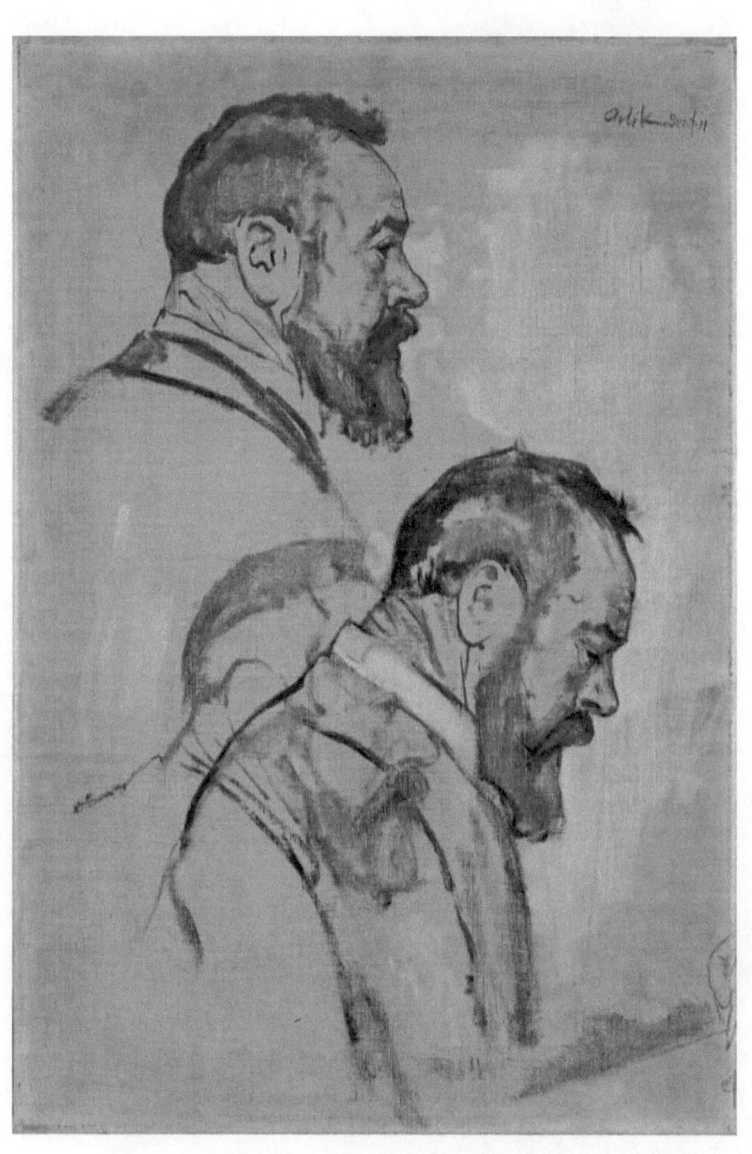

Studies of self-portrait
1911, oil

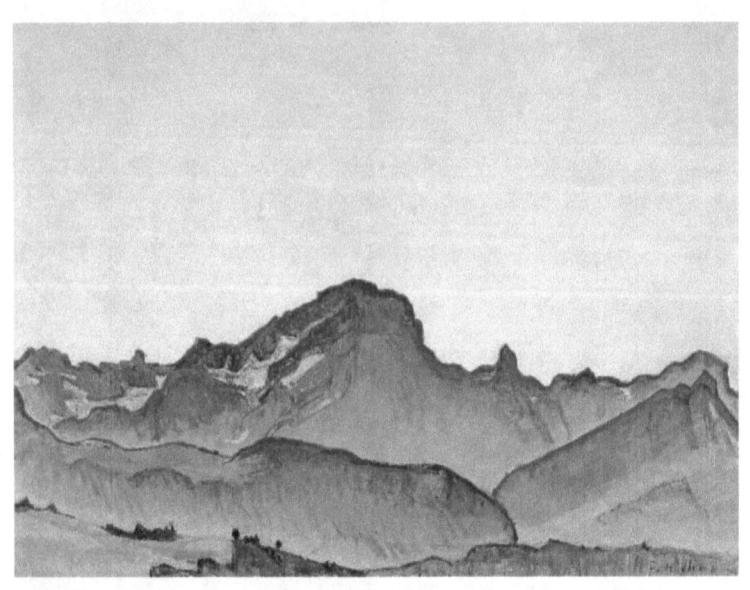

The Grand Muveran
1911, oil on canvas

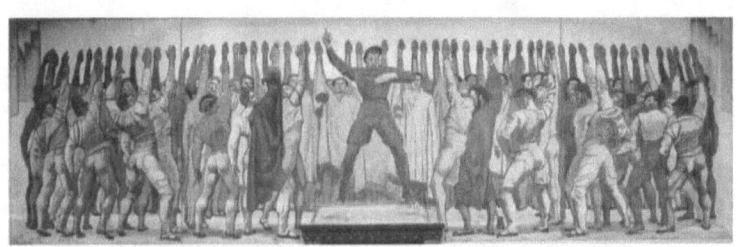

Unity
1911, oil on canvas

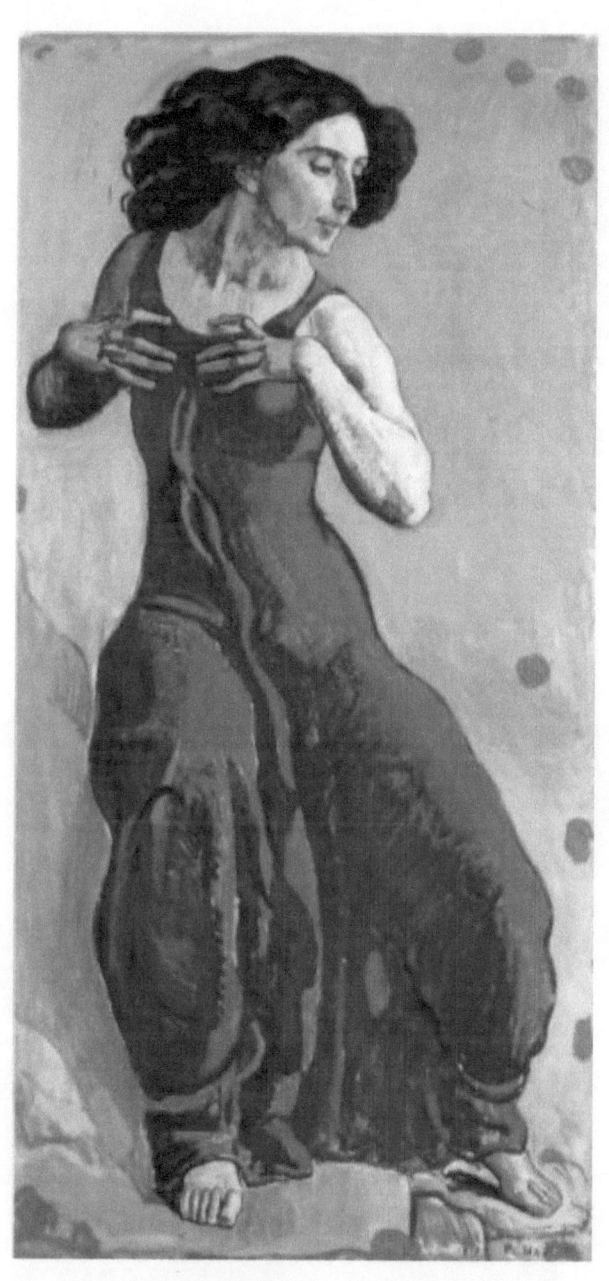

Woman in Ecstasy
1911, oil on canvas

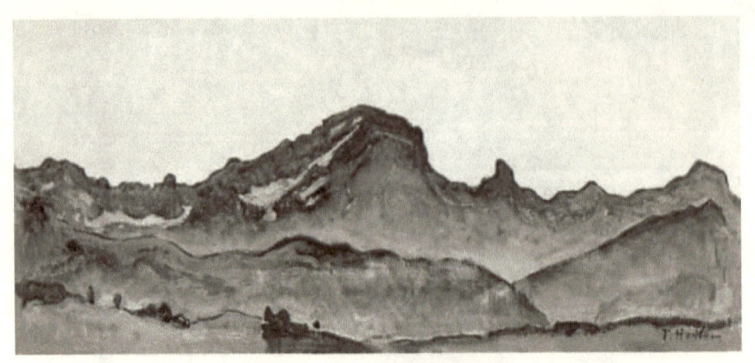

Grand Muveran
1912, oil on canvas

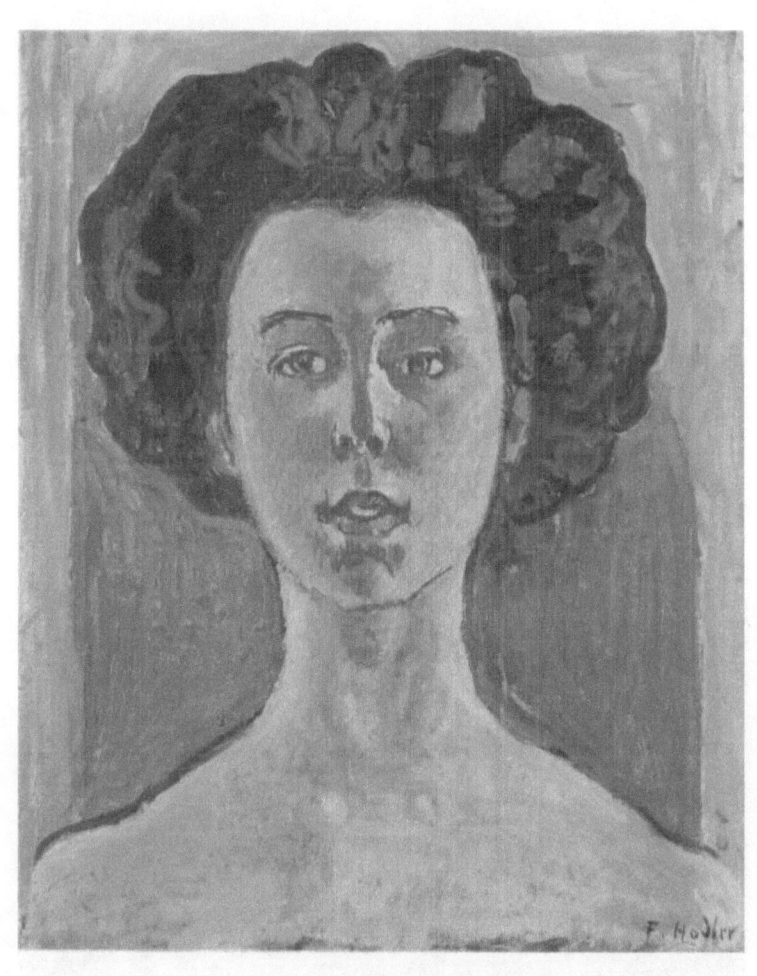

Portrait of Gertrud Mueller
1912, oil on canvas

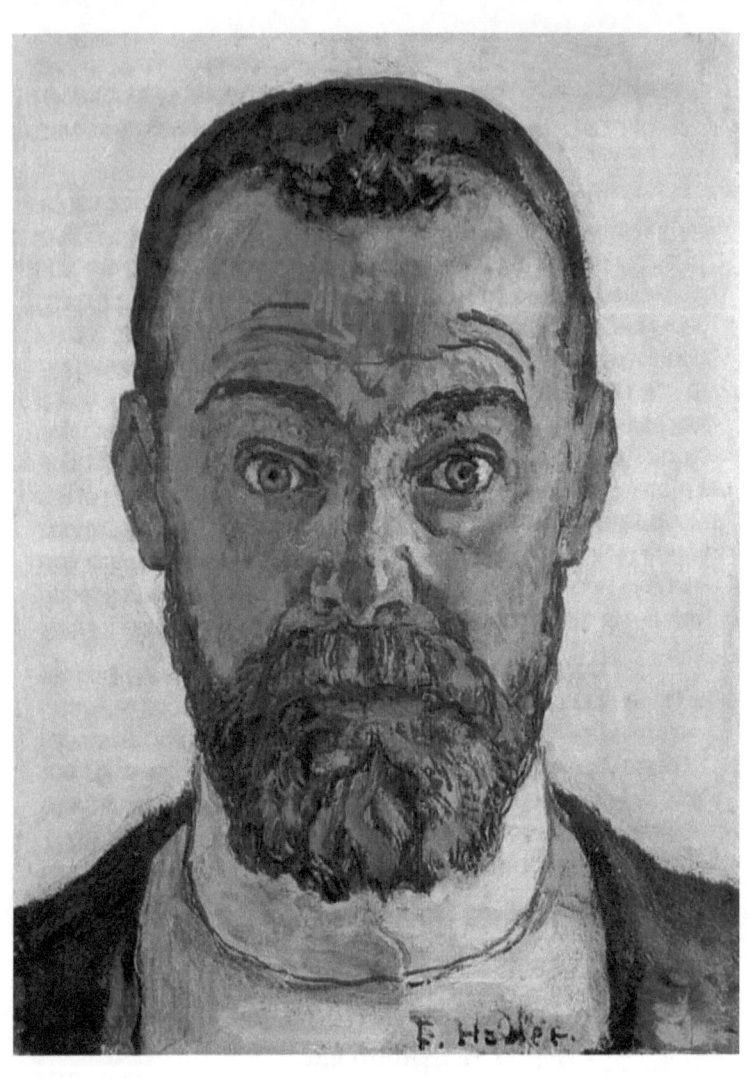

Self-portrait
1912, oil on canvas

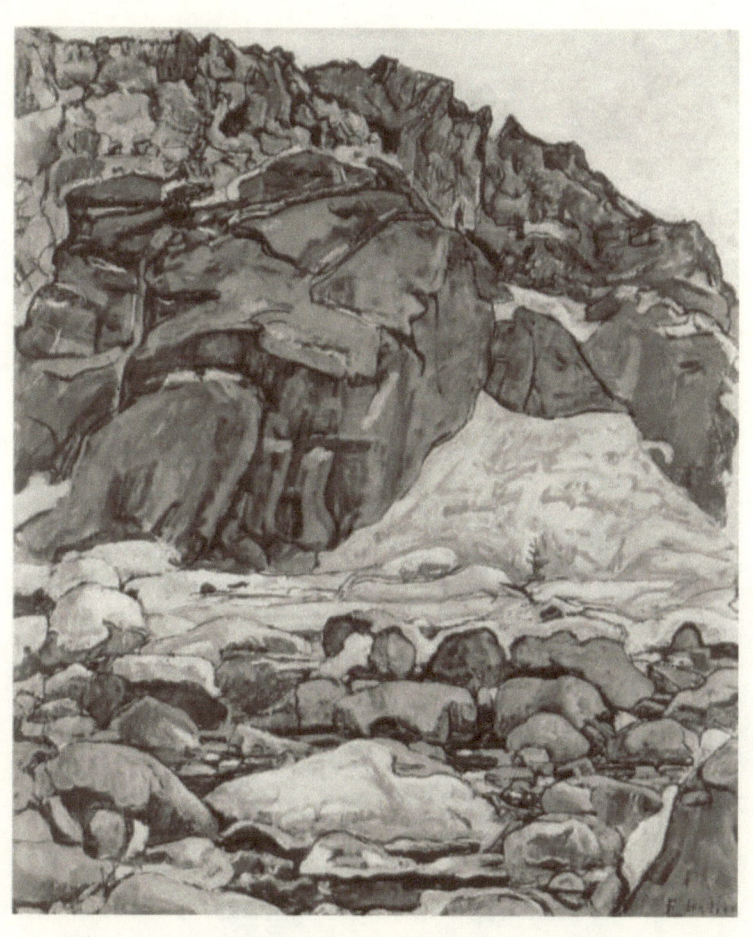

The Grindelwald glacier
1912, oil on canvas

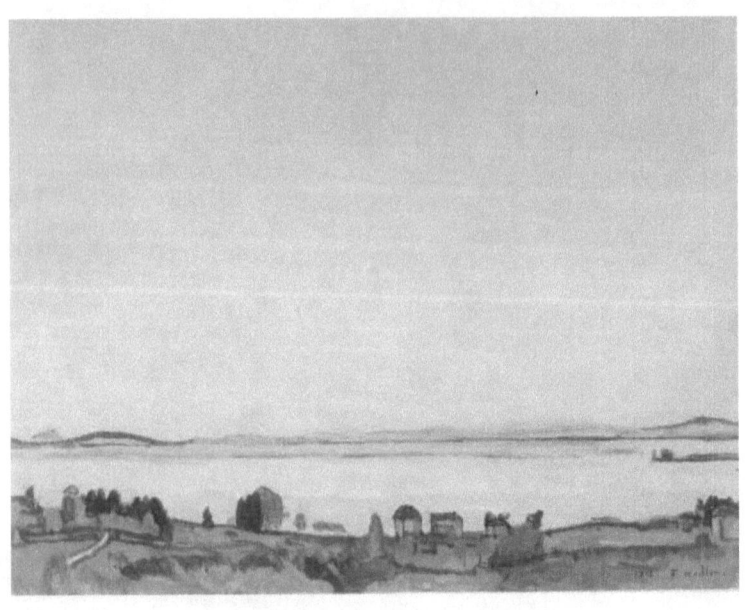

The Lake Geneva from Lausanne
1912, oil on canvas

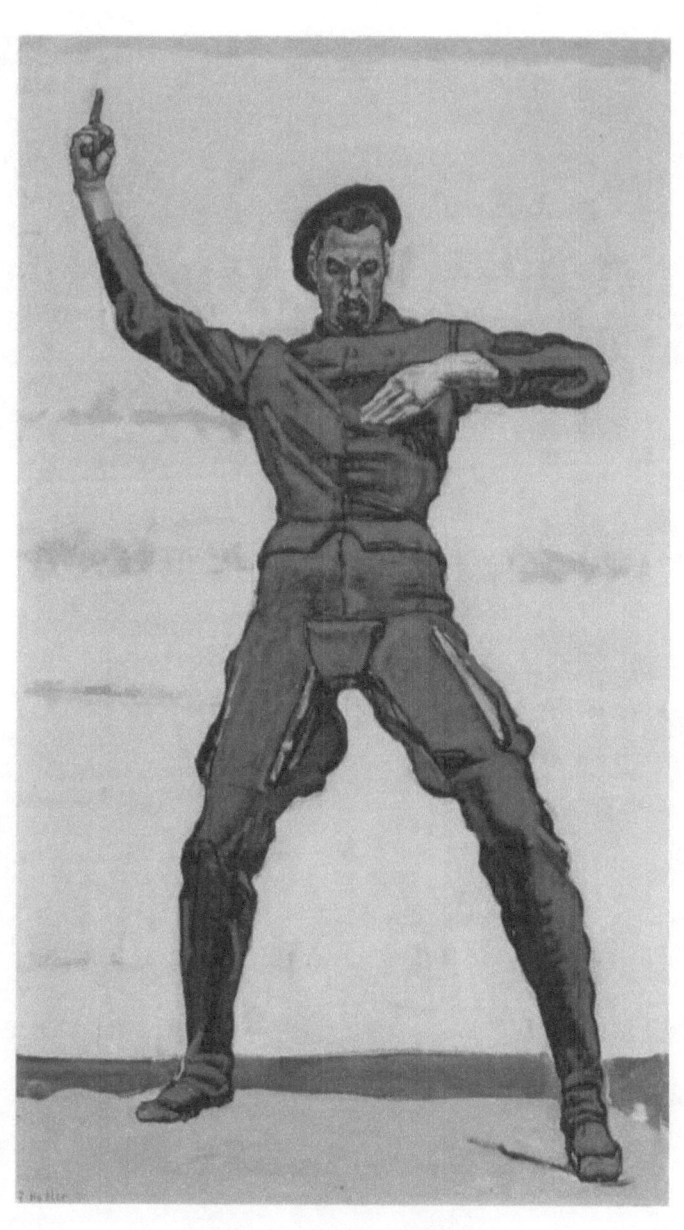

The Orator
1912, oil on canvas

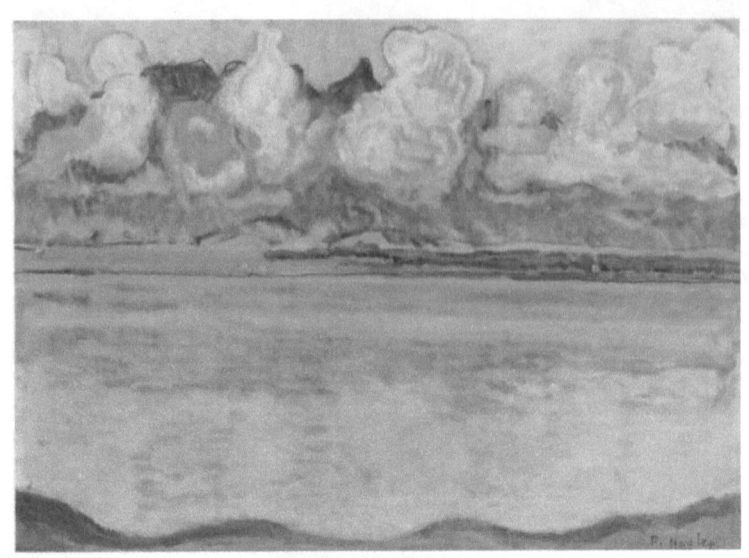

Thun, Stockhornkette, in clouds
1912, oil on canvas

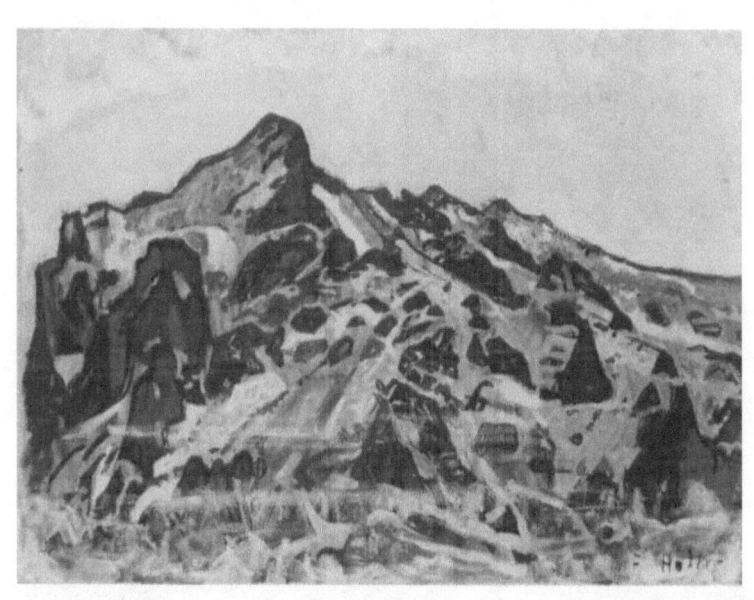

Wetterhorn
1912, oil on canvas

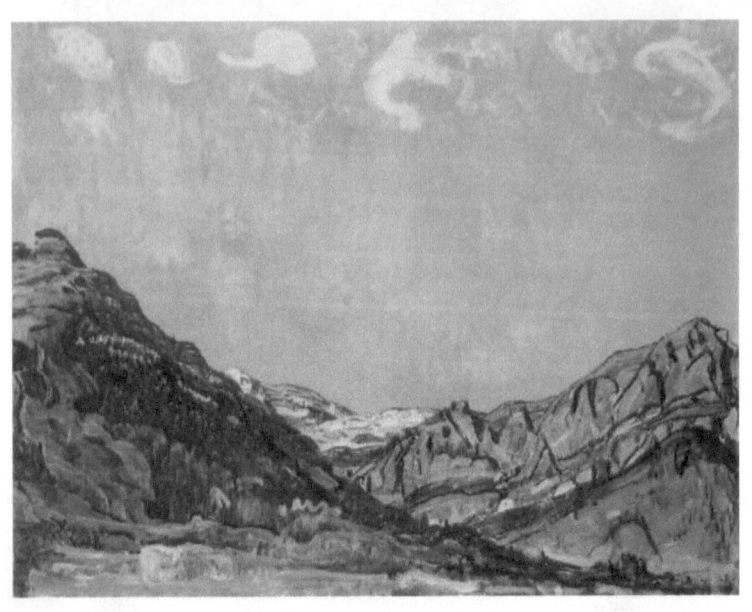

Landscape near Champery
1913, oil on canvas

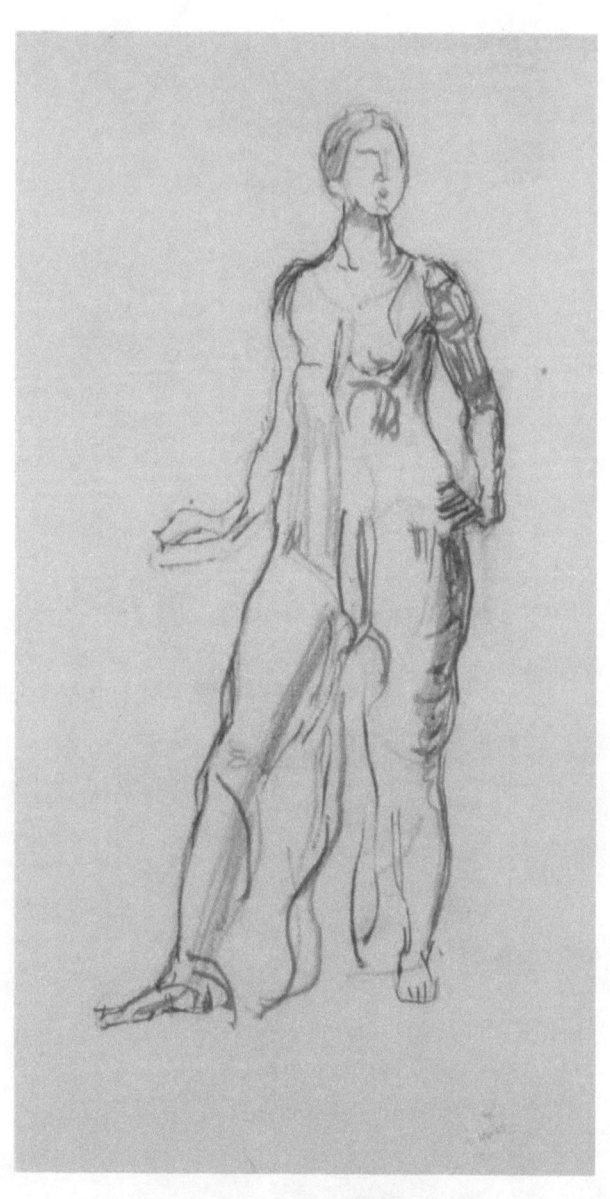

Standing draped figur
1913, pencil, watercolor

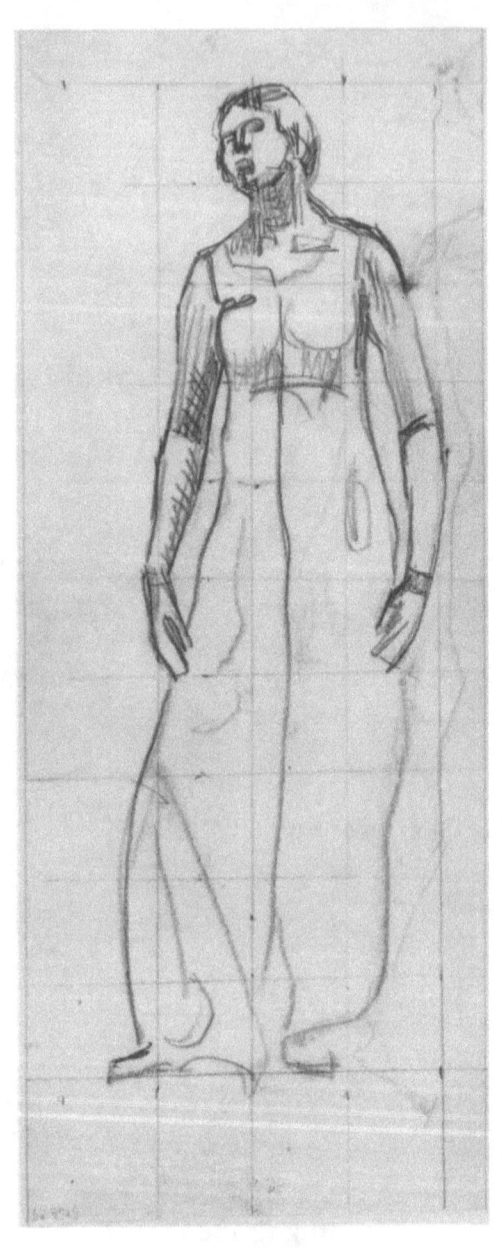

Standing draped figure
1913, pencil, watercolor

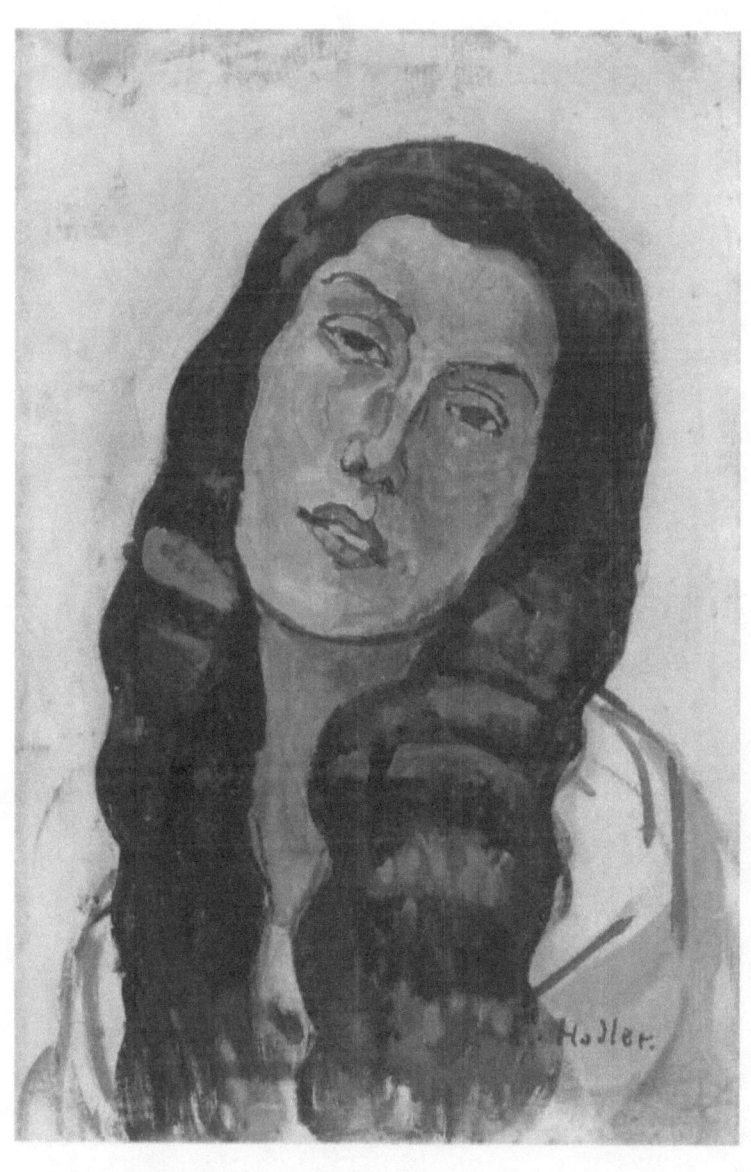

Valentine Gode Darel, with disheveled hair
1913, oil on canvas

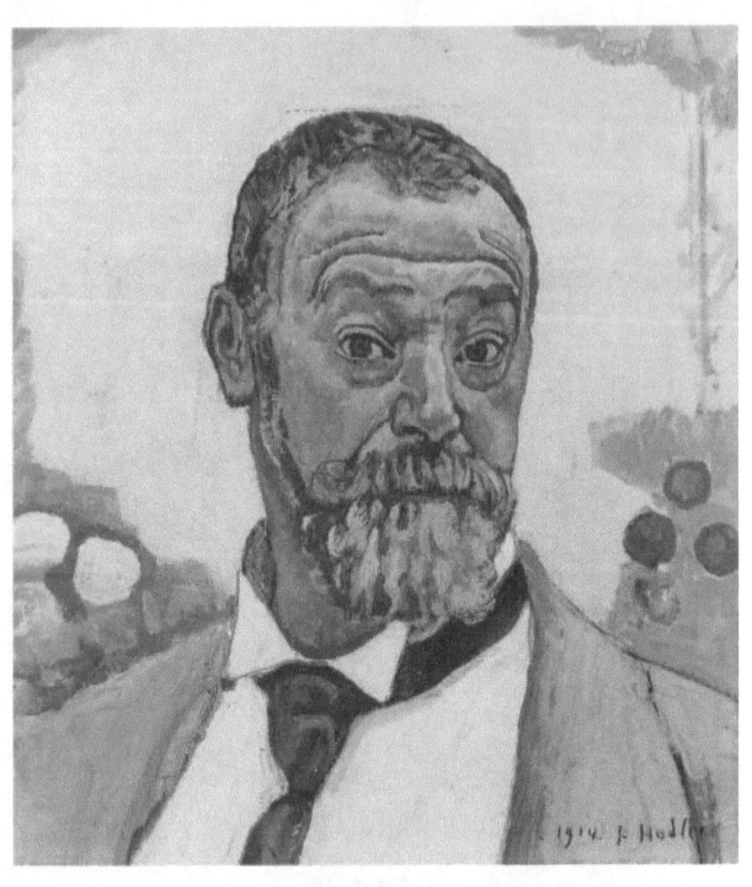

Self-portrait with roses
1914, oil on canvas

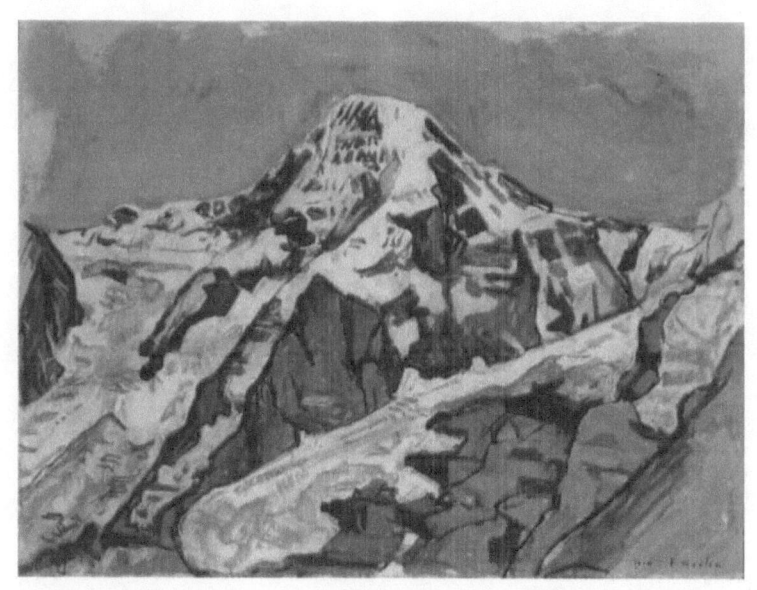

The Monk
1914, oil on canvas

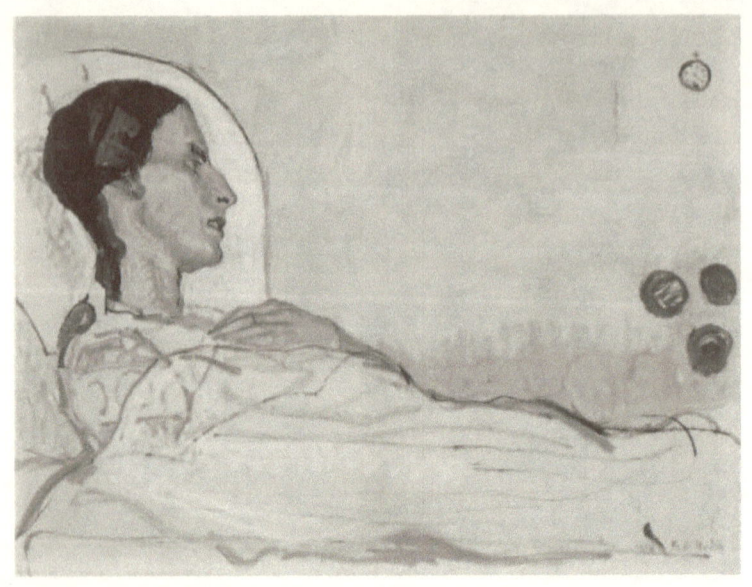

Valentine Gode Darel in hospital bed
1914, oil on canvas

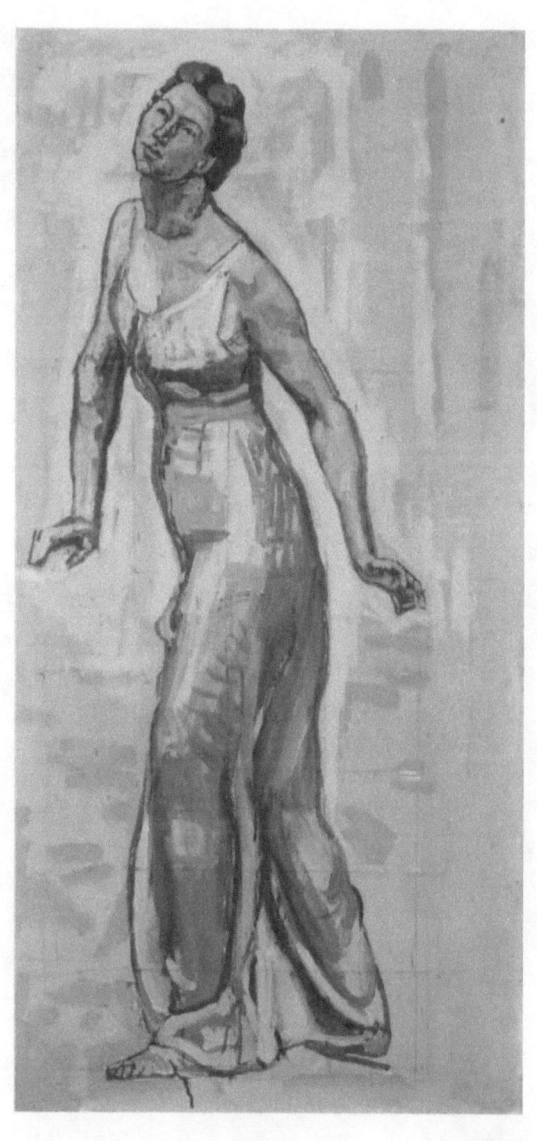

Border woman figure in blue Gwand
1915, oil on canvas

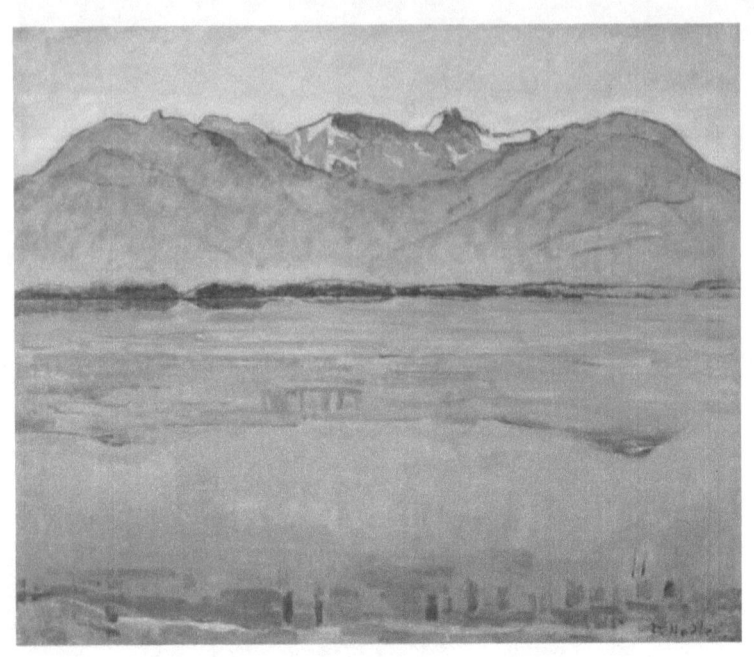

Montanasee
1915, oil on canvas

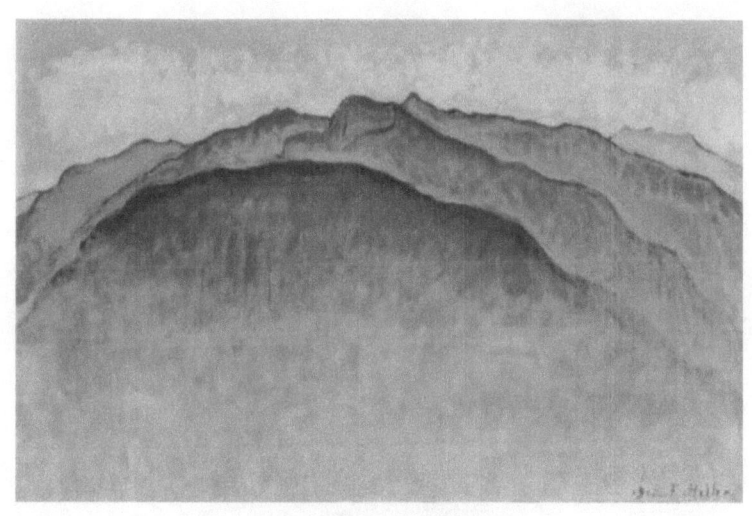

Peaks in the morning
1915, oil on canvas

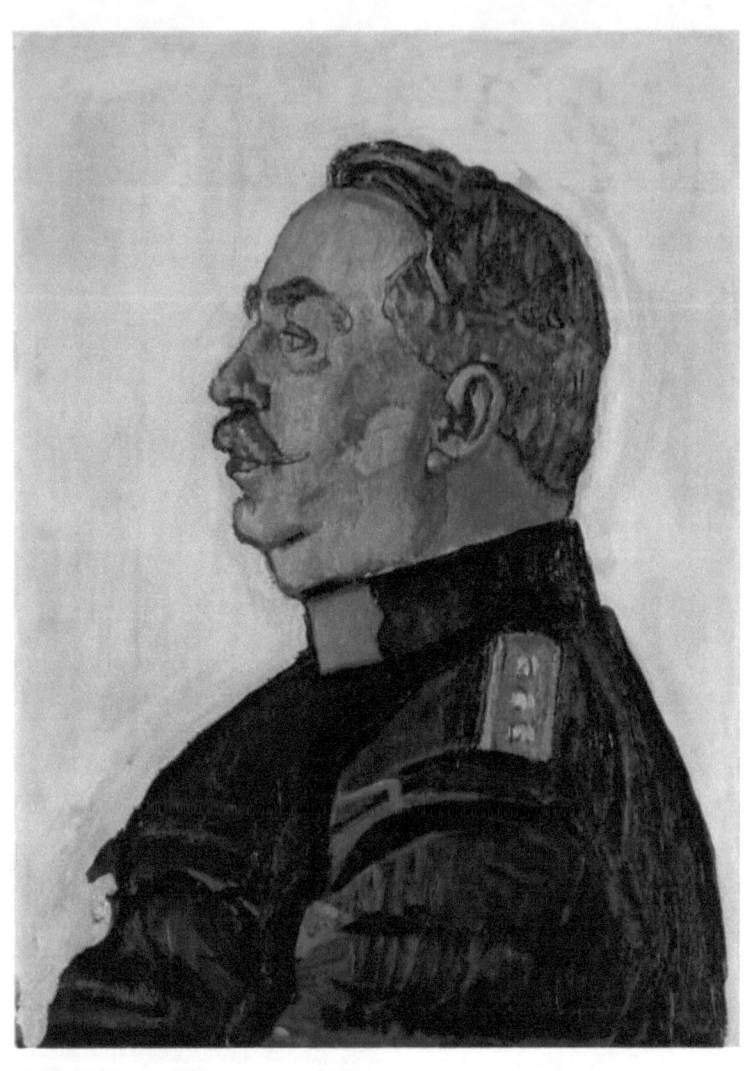

Portrait of General Ulrich Wille
1915, oil on canvas

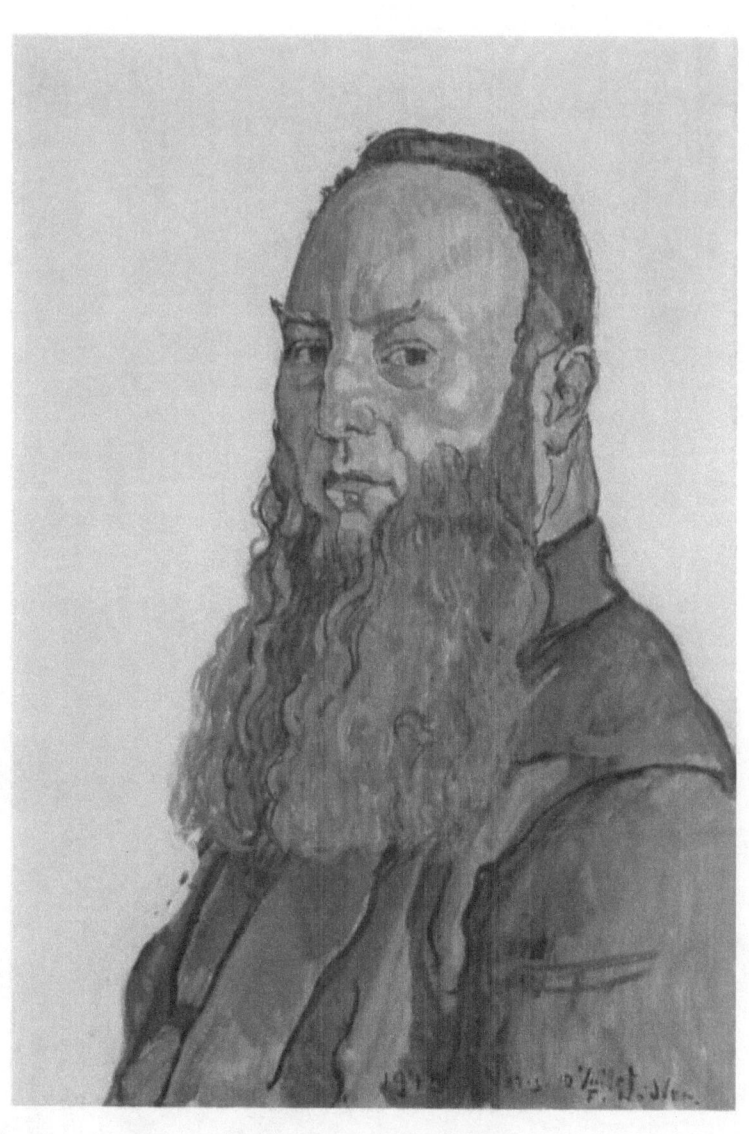

Portrait of James Vibert
1915, oil on canvas

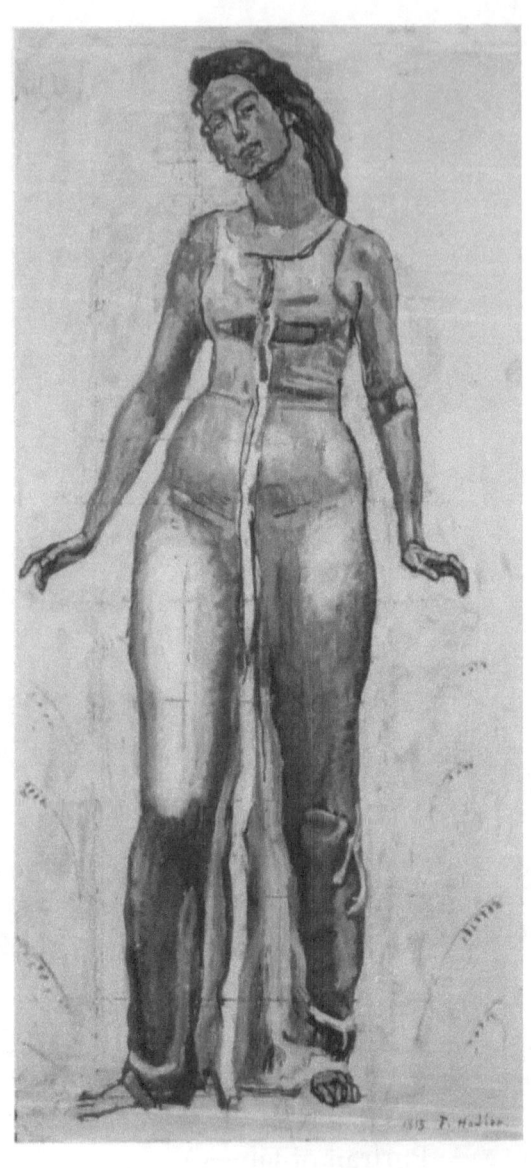

Standing female figure in a blue dress
1915, oil on canvas

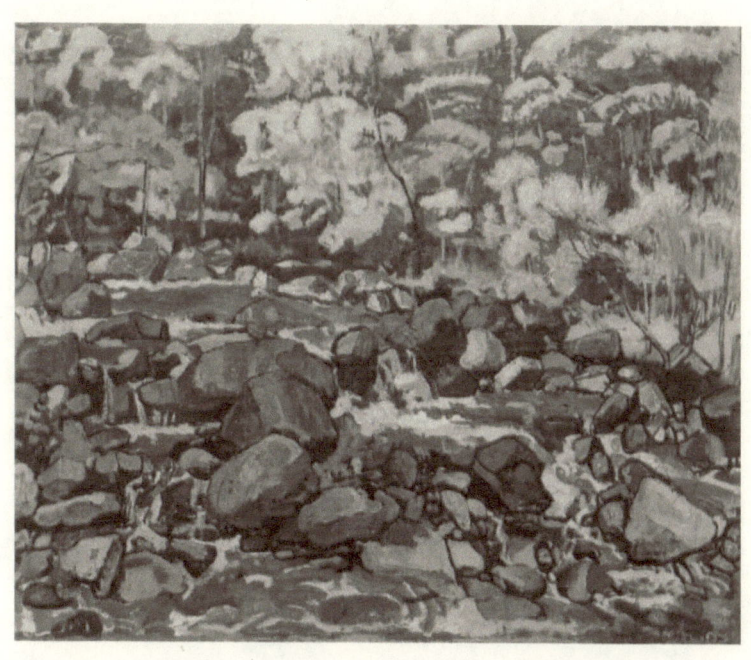

Forest Stream at Champery
1916, oil on canvas

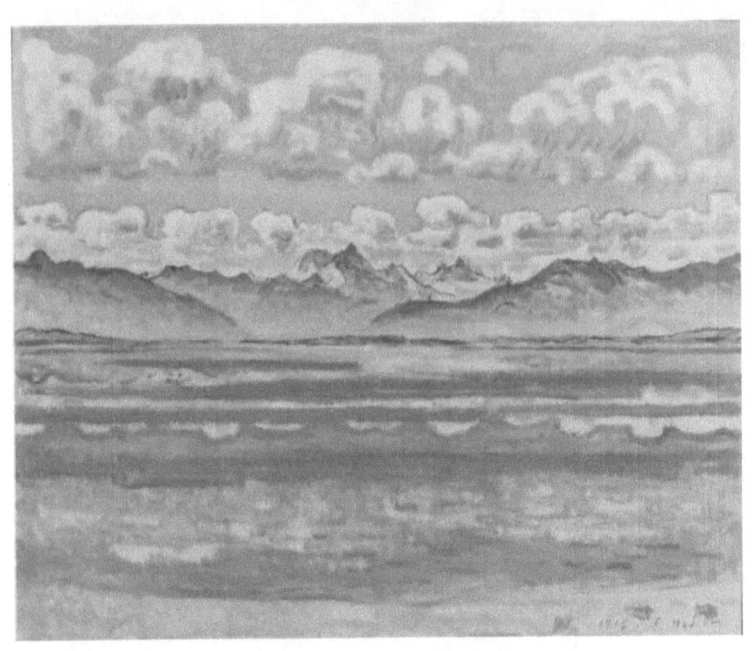

Weisshorn of Montana
1916, oil on canvas

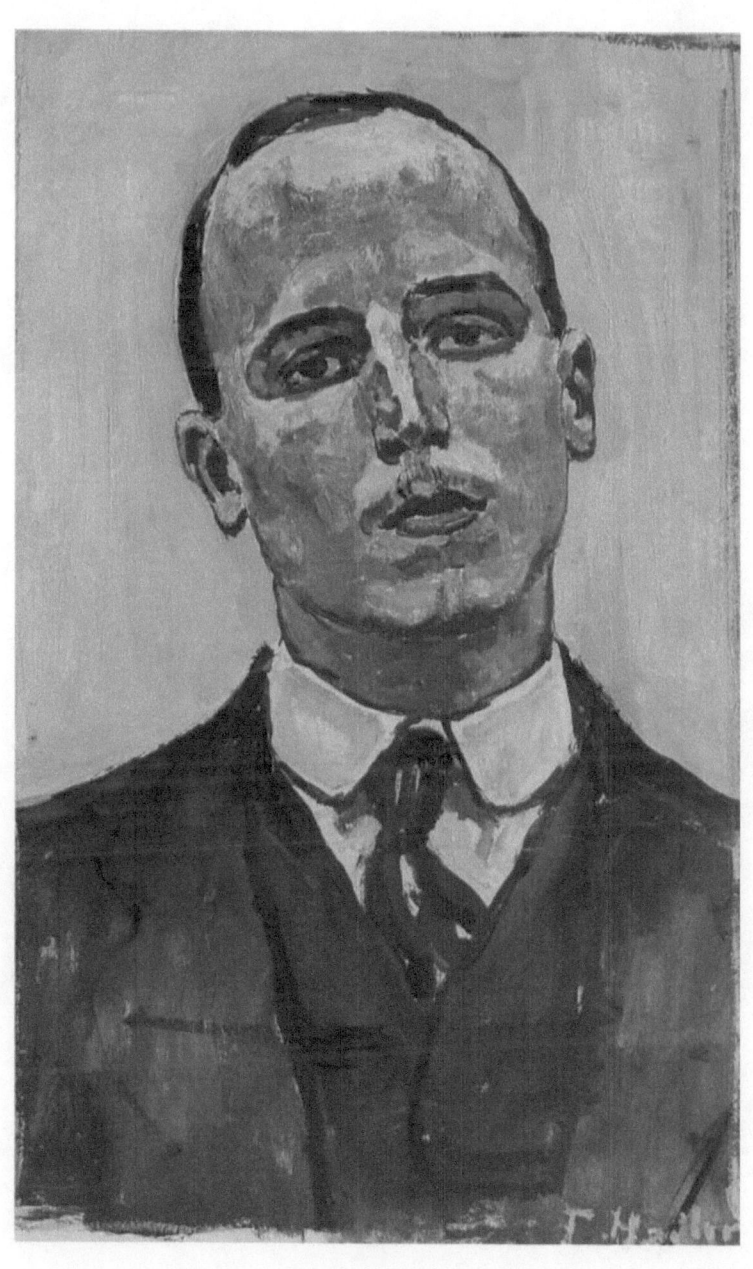

Josef Müller
1916, oil on canvas

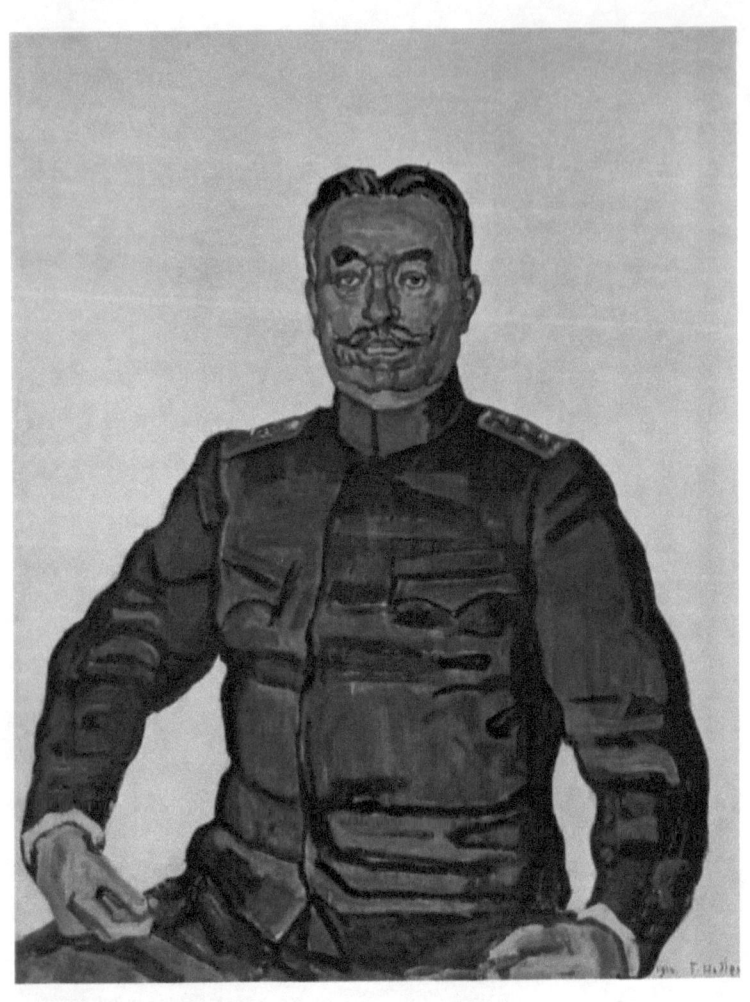

Portrait of General Ulrich Wille
1916, oil on canvas

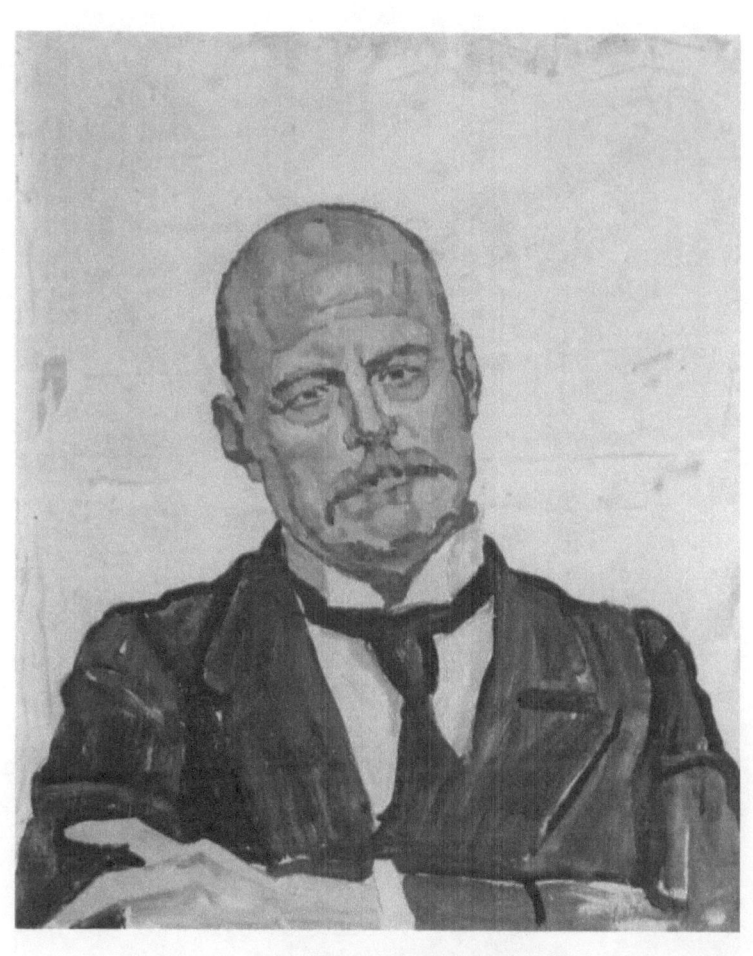

Portrait of Georges Navazza
1916, oil on canvas

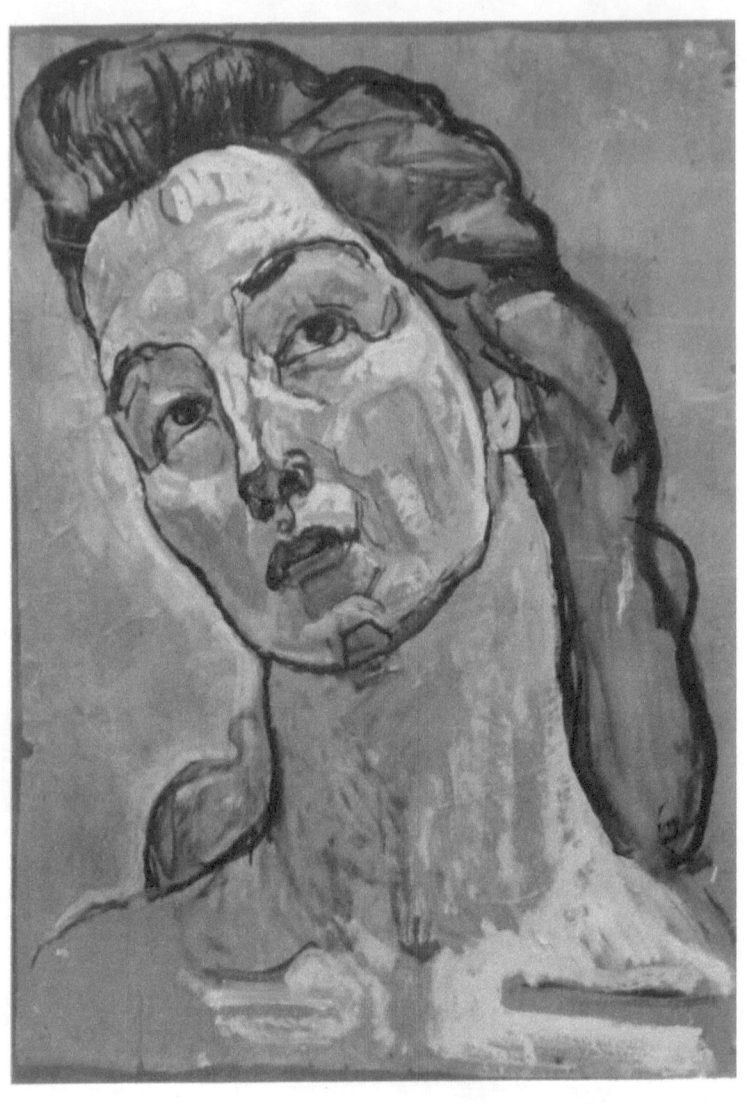

Portrait study to "Look into the infinity"
1916, oil on canvas

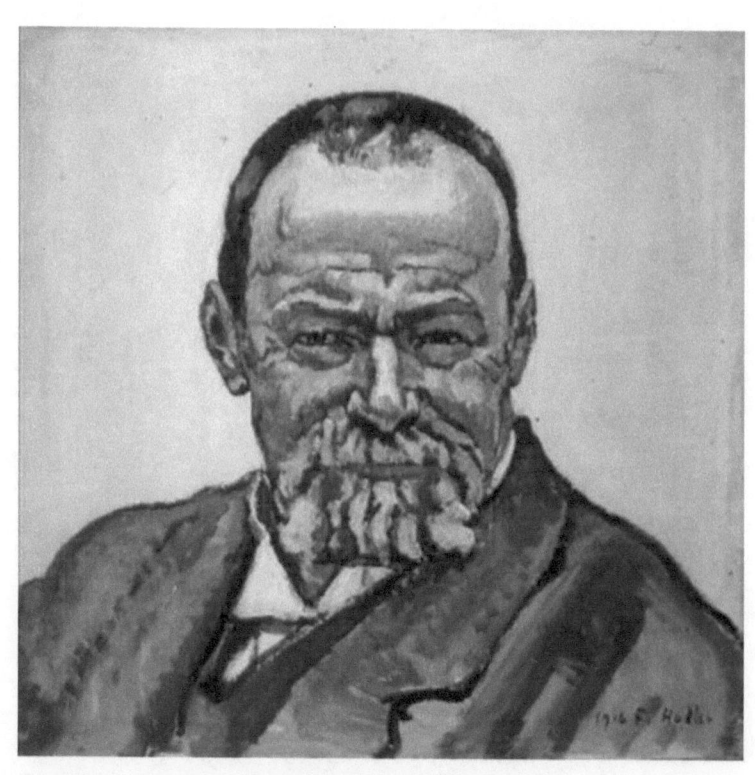

Self portrait
1916, oil on canvas

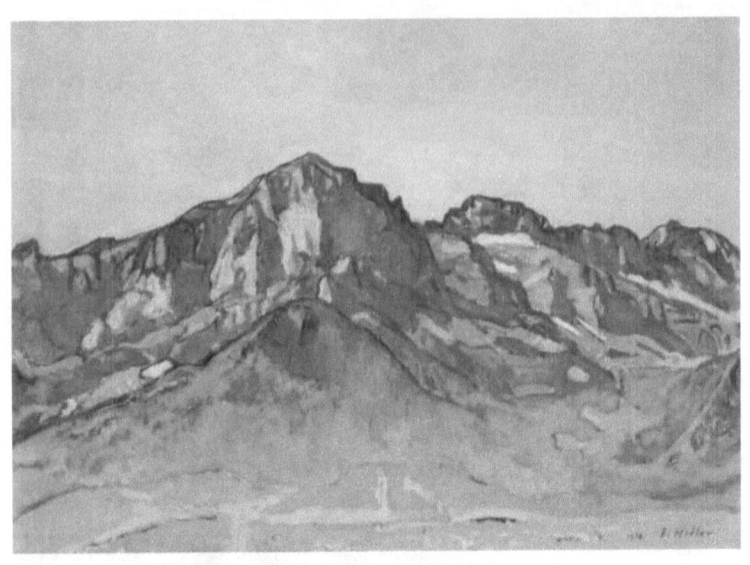

The Dents Blanches in Champéry at the morning sun
1916, oil on canvas

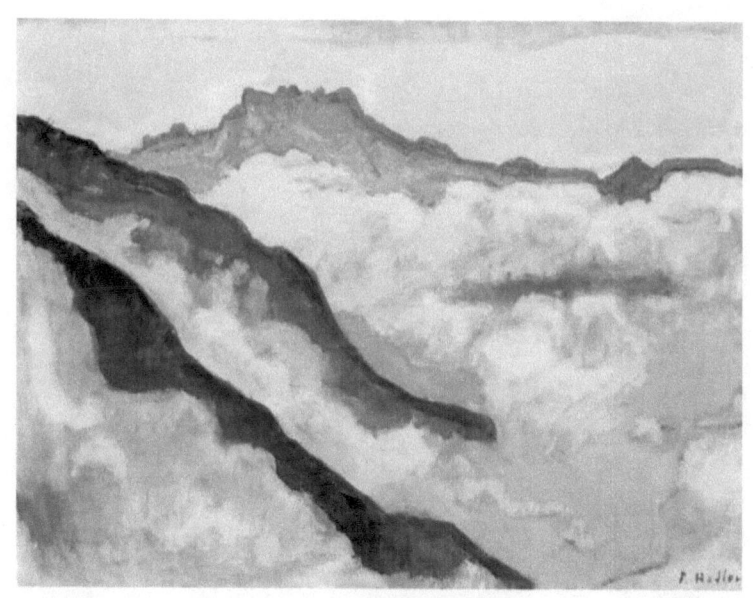

Dents du Midi in Clouds
1916, oil on canvas

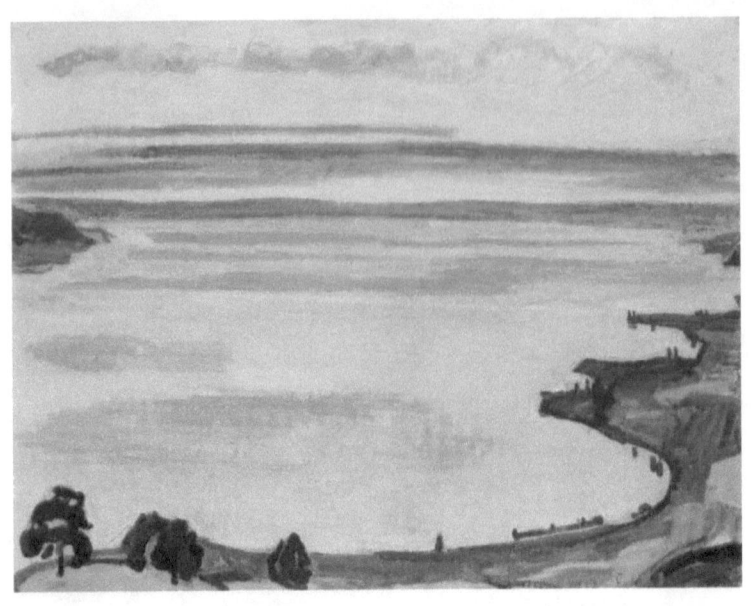

Sunset on Lake Geneva from the Caux
1916, oil on canvas

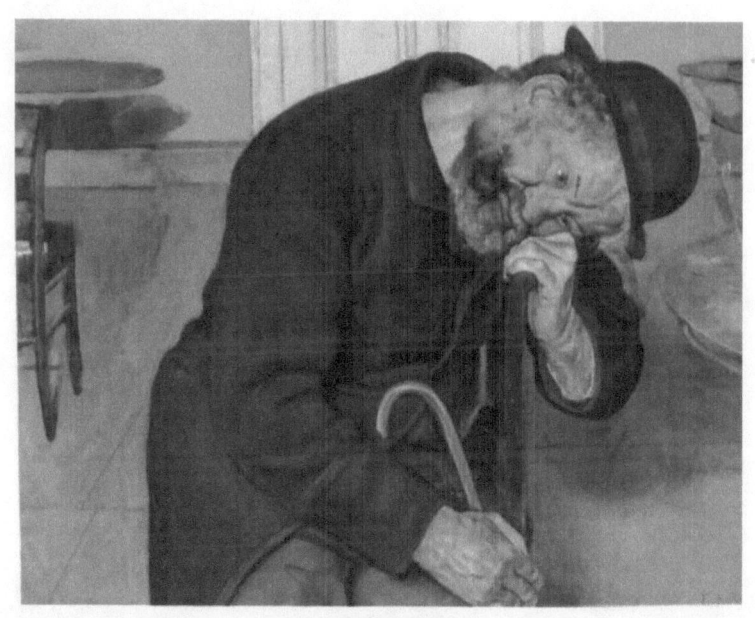

A Troubled Soul
N.d., oil on canvas

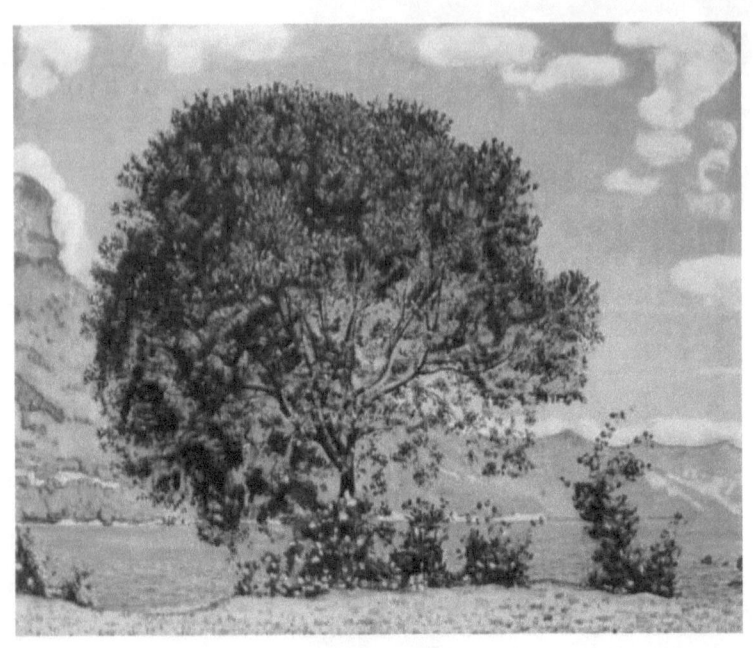

A View of Lake Brienz from Bodeli
N.d., oil on canvas

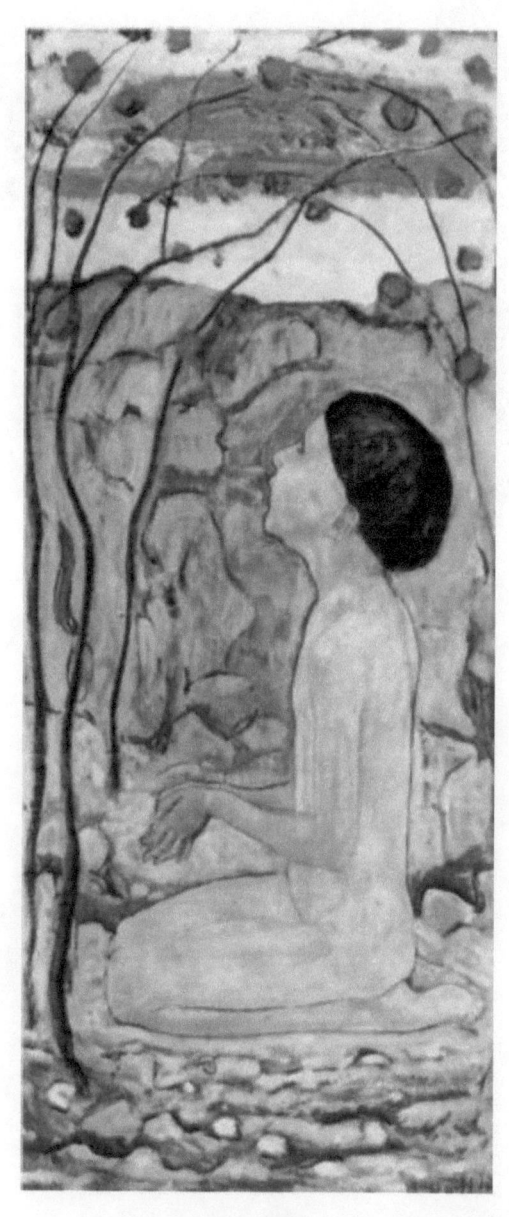

Adoration
N.d., oil on canvas

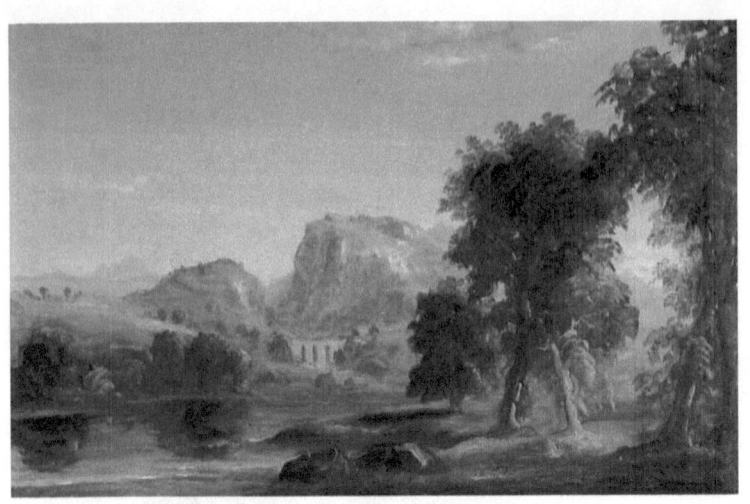

Dream
N.d., oil on canvas

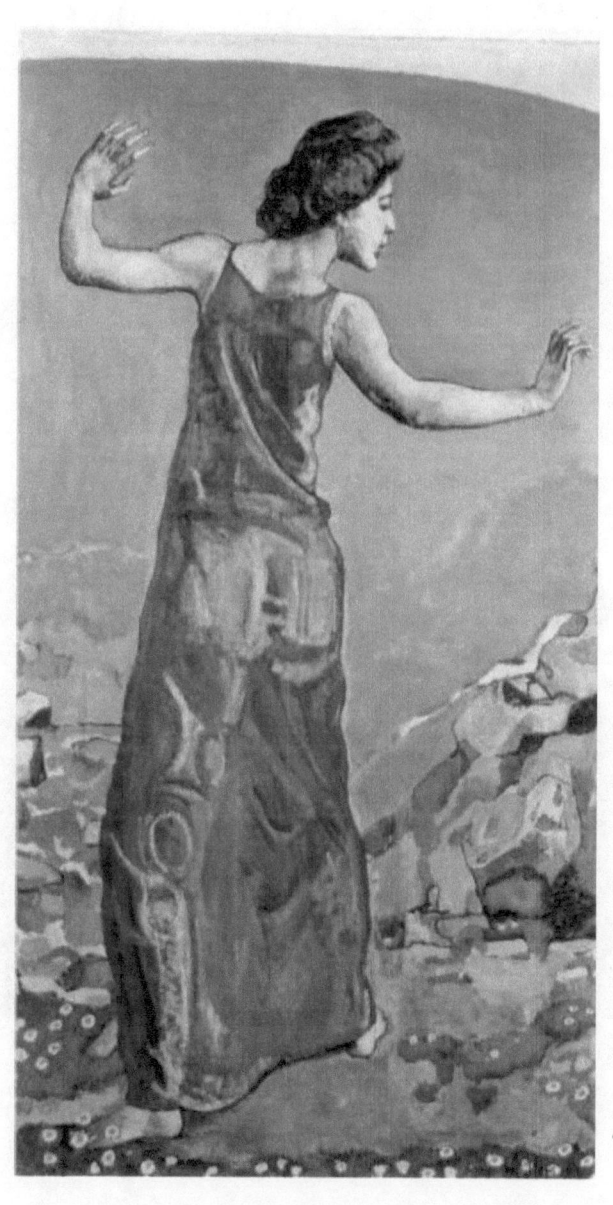

Joyous Woman
N.d., oil on canvas

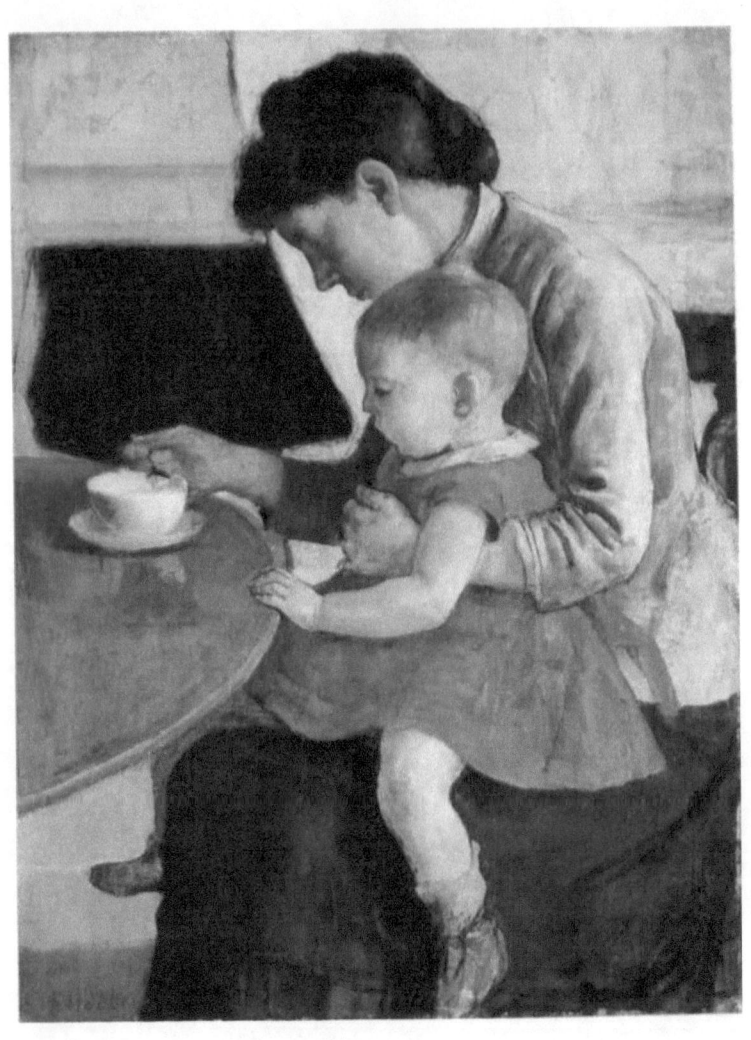

Mother and Child
N.d., oil on canvas

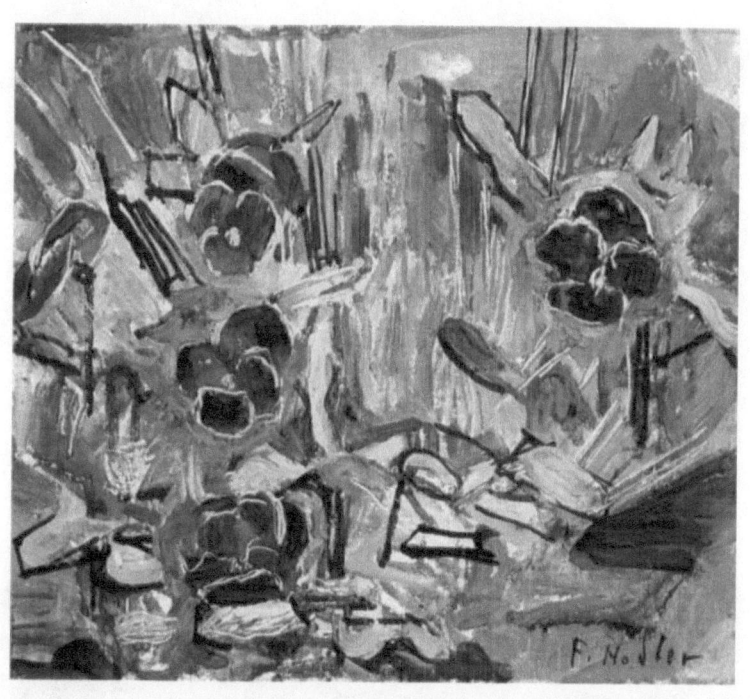

Pansies
N.d., oil on canvas

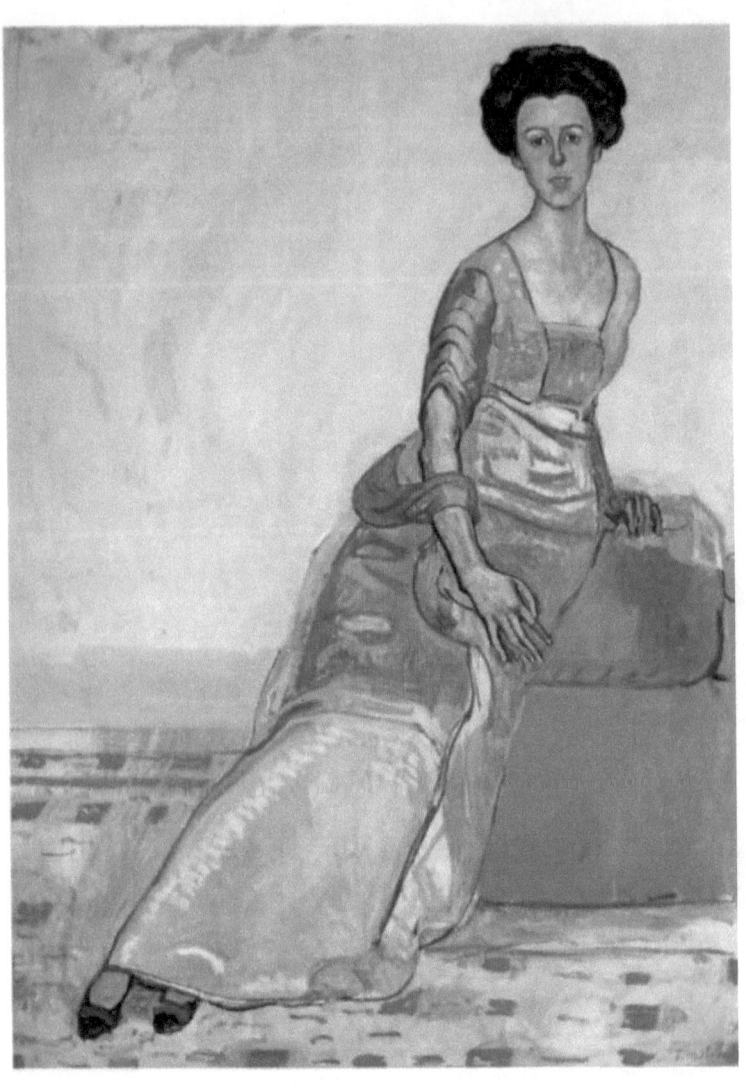

Portrait of Gertrud Muller
N.d., oil on canvas

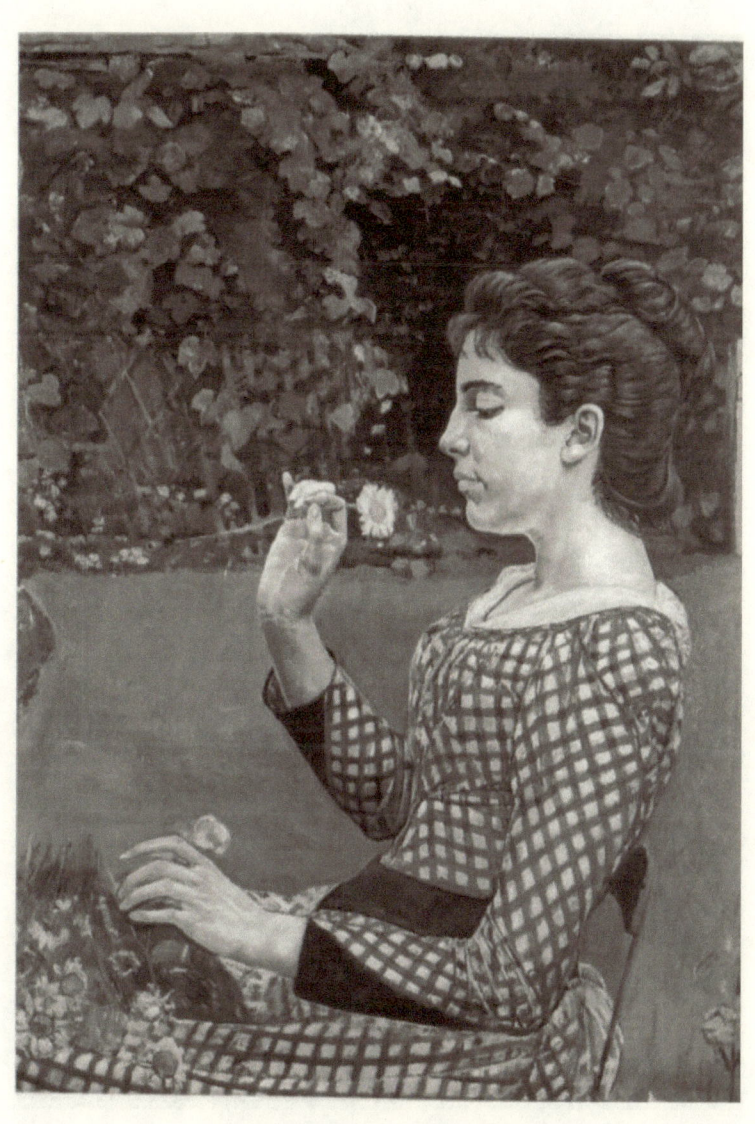

Portrait of Helene Weigle
N.d., oil on canvas

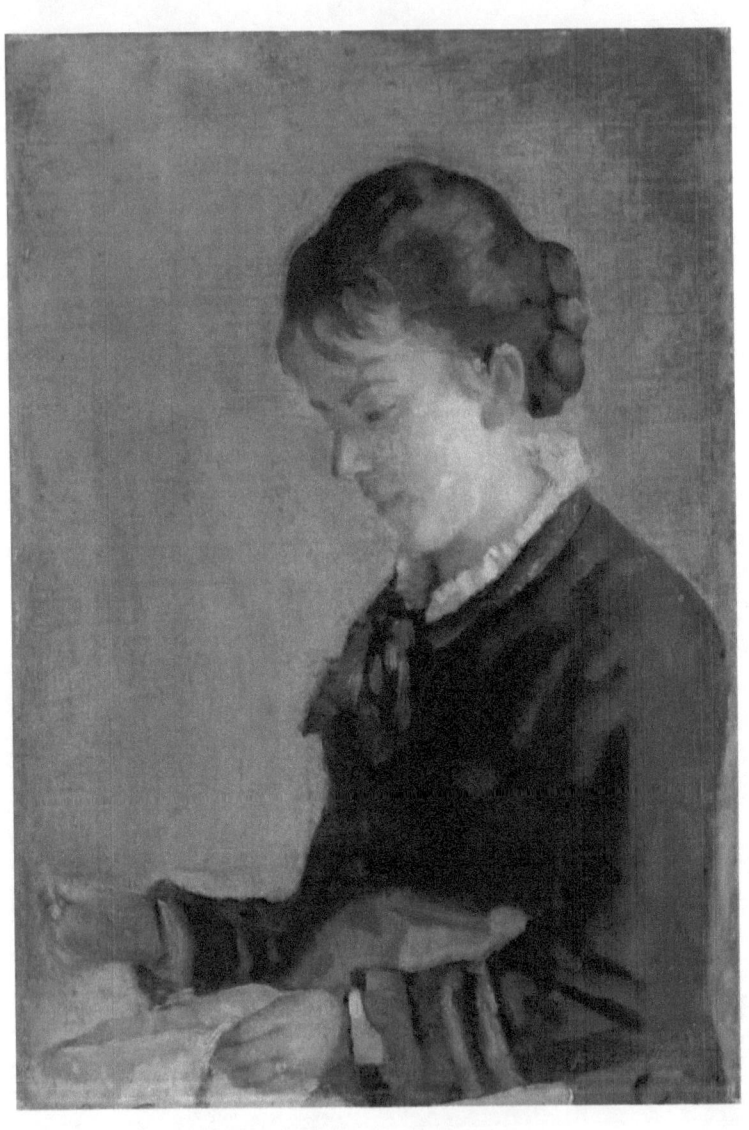

Portrait of Miss Lina Kyburz
N.d., oil on canvas

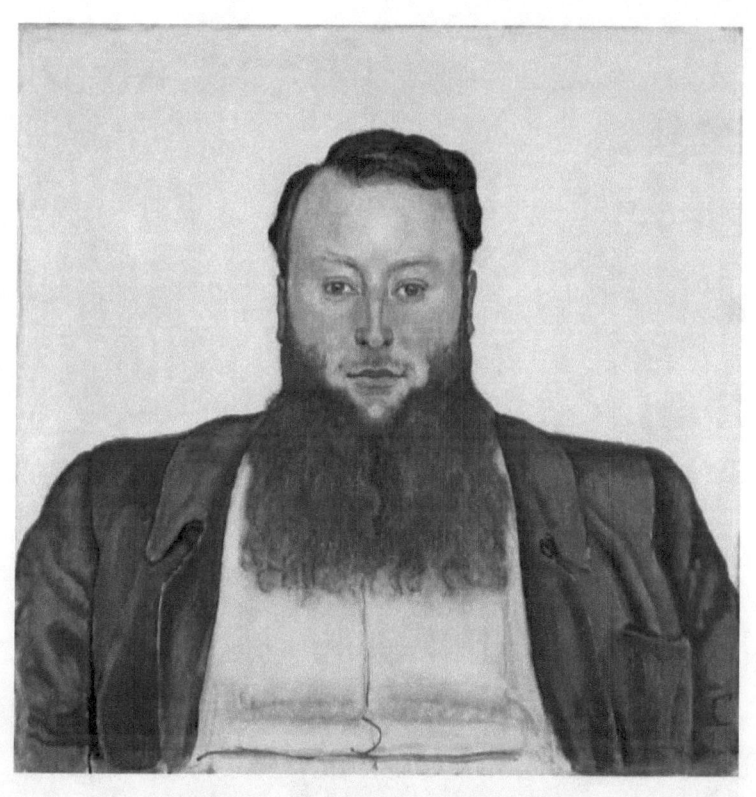

Portrait of sculptor James Vibert
N.d., oil on canvas

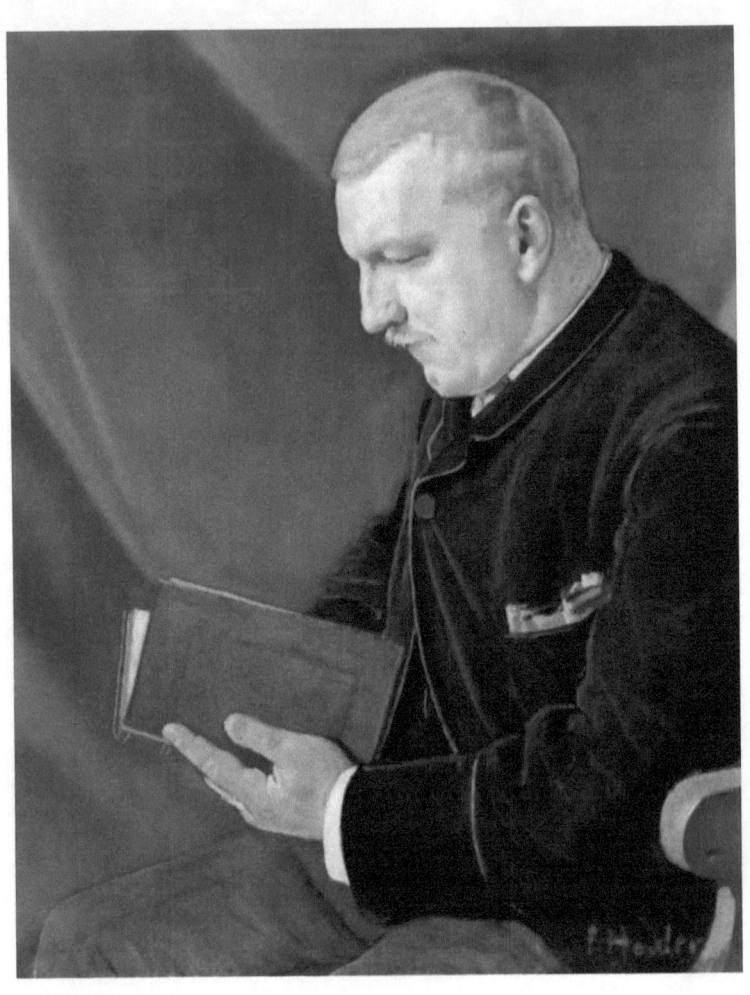

Reading-man
N.d., oil on canvas

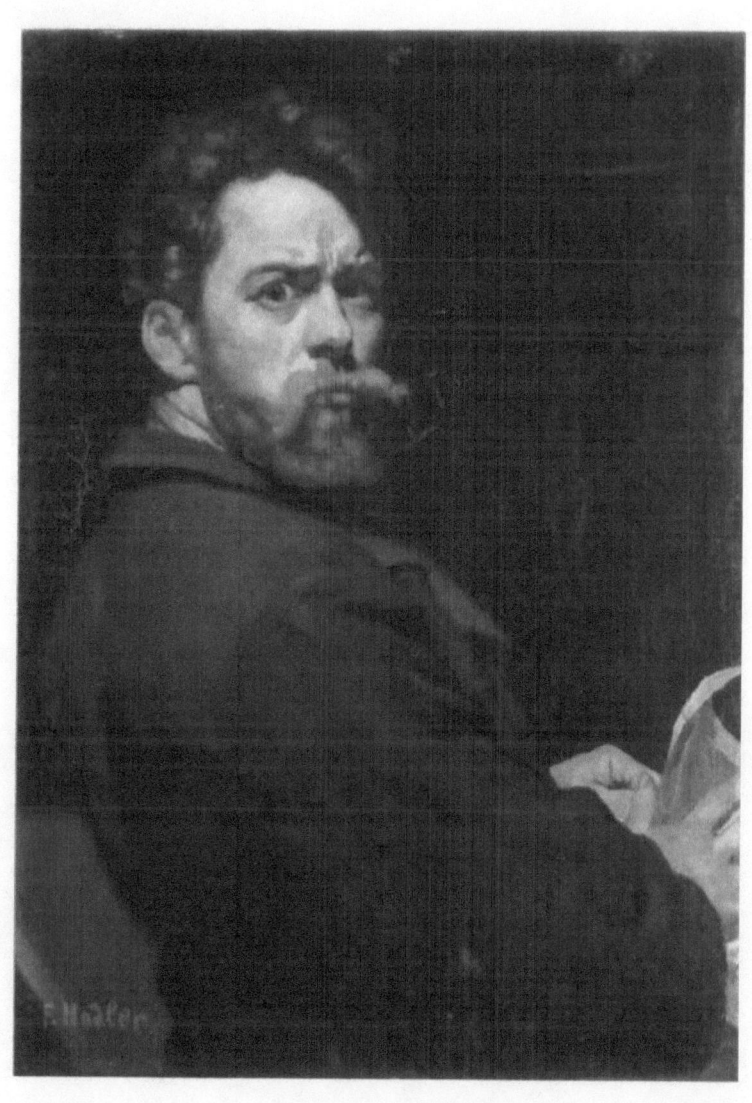

The Angry One
N.d., oil on canvas

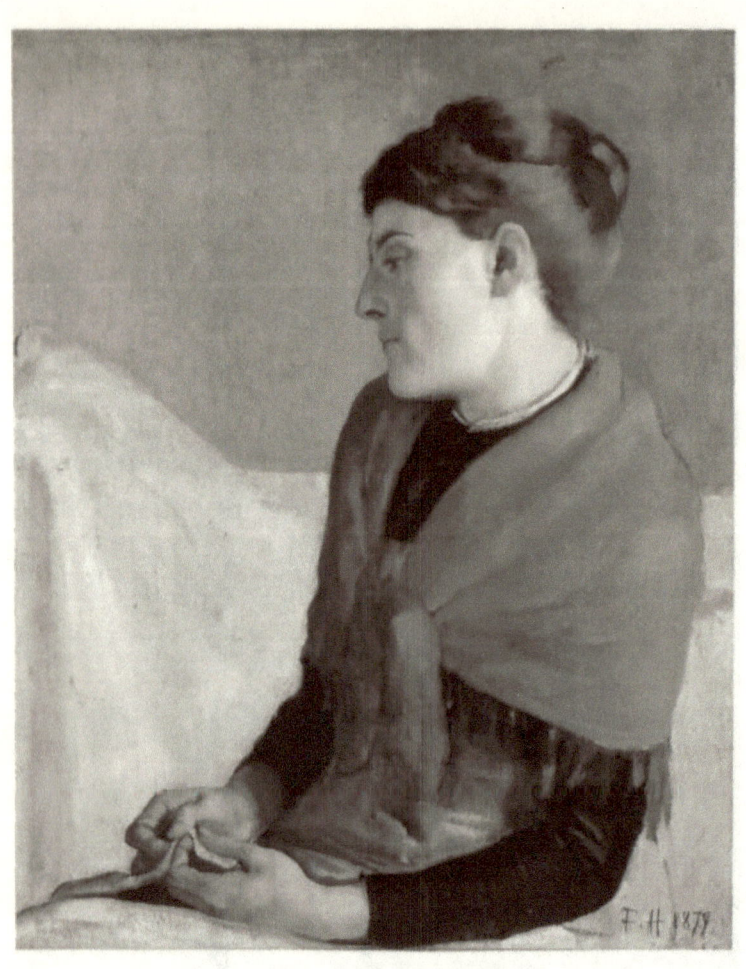

The Convalescent
N.d., oil on canvas

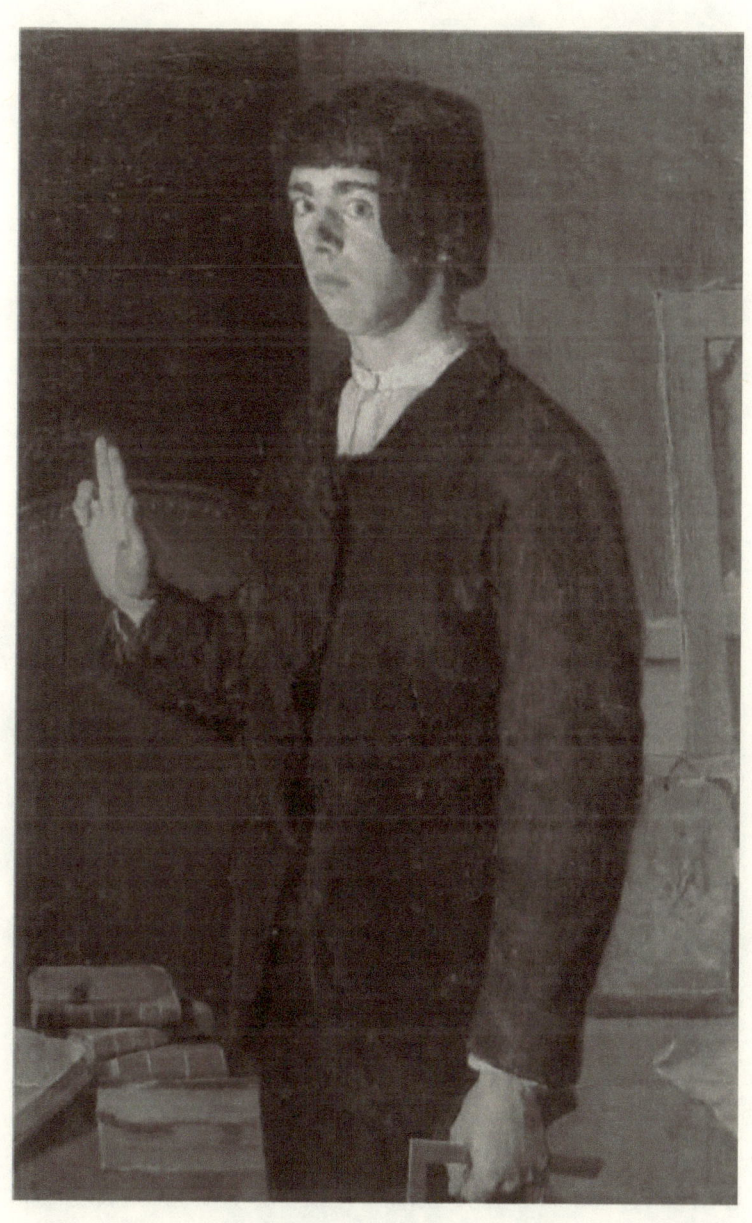

The student (Self-portrait)
N.d., oil on canvas

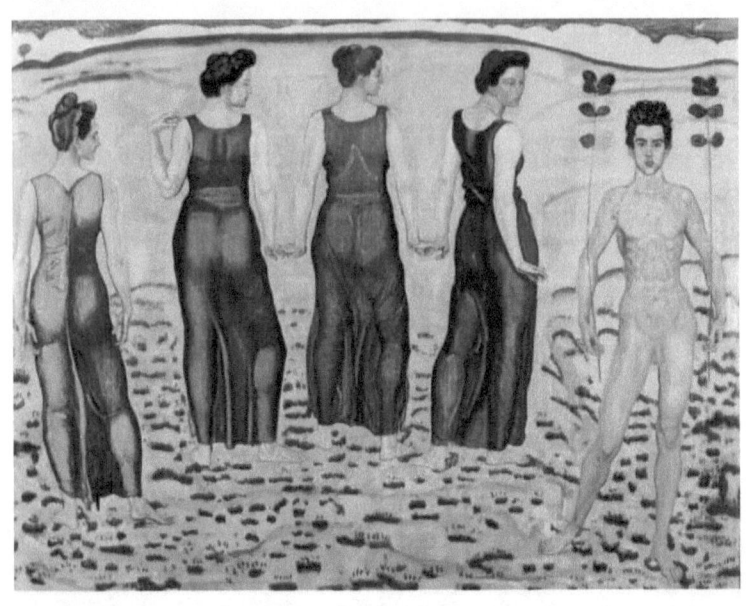

Youth Admired by Women
N.d., oil on canvas

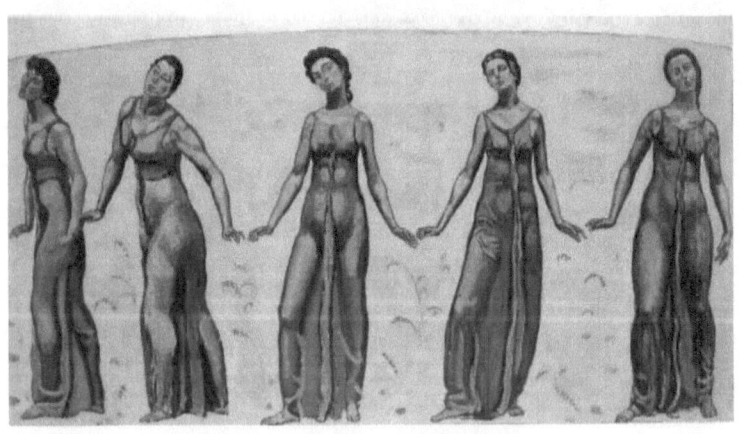

View into Infinity
N.d., oil on canvas